The Mother

WORDS OF LONG AGO

SRI AUROBINDO ASHRAM
PONDICHERRY

First edition 1946
Fourth edition (enlarged) 1994
Third impression 2005

Rs. 40.00
ISBN 81-7058-377-2

Published by Sri Aurobindo Ashram Publication Department,
Pondicherry - 605 002
Website: http://sabda.sriaurobindoashram.org
Printed at Sri Aurobindo Ashram Press, Pondicherry
PRINTED IN INDIA

Contents

Contents

Publisher's Note

This book contains early writings of the Mother – writings from the period before 1920, the year she finally settled in Pondicherry. It is divided into four parts according to the nature and date of the material.

Part 1 consists of stories, talks and reflections written between 1893 and 1913, Part 2 of nine essays written for the meetings of "a small group of seekers" in 1912, Part 3 of four talks delivered between 1911 and 1913, and Part 4 of letters and essays written in Japan between 1916 and 1920.

This edition is an enlarged version of the book of the same title first published in 1946 and subsequently in 1952 and 1974. The new material is taken from Volume 2 of the Mother's Collected Works, also entitled *Words of Long Ago*, which was published in 1978. The text has been reproduced by photo-offset from pages of Volume 2.

THE MOTHER
Tokyo 1916

THE MOTHER
1879-1914

PART 1

The Path of Later On

"The path of later-on and the road of tomorrow
lead only to the castle of nothing-at-all."

By the wayside, many-coloured flowers delight the eye, red berries gleam on small trees with knotty branches, and in the distance a brilliant sun shines gold upon the ripe corn.

A young traveller is walking briskly along, happily breathing in the pure morning air; he seems joyful, without a care for the future. The way he is following comes to a cross-roads, where innumerable paths branch off in all directions.

Everywhere the young man can see criss-crossing foot-prints. The sun shines ever bright in the sky; the birds are singing in the trees; the day promises to be very beautiful. Without thinking, the traveller takes the path that is nearest to him, which seems, after all, quite practicable; it occurs to him for a moment that he could have chosen another way; but there will always be time to retrace his steps if the path he has taken leads nowhere. A voice seems to tell him, "Turn back, turn back, you are not on the right road." But everything around him is charming and delightful. What should he do ? He does not know. He goes on without taking any decision; he enjoys the pleasures of the moment. "In a little while," he replies to the voice, "in a little while I shall think; I have plenty of time." The wild grasses around him whisper in his ear, "Later." Later, yes, later. Ah, how pleasant it is to breathe the scented breeze, while the sun warms the air with its fiery rays. Later, later. And the traveller walks on; the path widens. Voices are heard from afar, "Where are you going ? Poor fool, don't you see that you are heading for your ruin ? You are young; come, come to us, to the beautiful, the good, the true; do not be misled by indolence and weakness; do not fall asleep in the present; come to the future." "Later, later," the traveller answers these unwelcome voices. The

3

flowers smile at him and echo, "Later." The path becomes wider and wider. The sun has reached its zenith; it is a glorious day. The path becomes a road.

The road is white and dusty, bordered with slender birch-trees; the soft purling of a little stream is heard; but in vain he looks in every direction, he can see no end to this interminable road.

The young man, feeling a secret unease, cries, "Where am I ? Where am I going ?... What does it matter ? Why think, why act ? Let us drift along on this endless road; let us walk on, I shall think tomorrow."

The small trees have disappeared; oak-trees line the road; a gully runs on either side. The traveller feels no weariness; he is borne along as if in a delirium.

The gully becomes deeper; the oaks give way to fir-trees; the sun begins to go down. In a daze, the traveller looks all around him; he sees human figures rolling into the ravine, clutching at the fir-trees, the sheer rocks, the roots jutting from the ground. Some of them are making great efforts to climb out; but as they come near to the edge, they turn their heads and let themselves fall back.

Hollow voices cry out to the traveller, "Flee this place; go back to the cross-roads; there is still time." The young man hesitates, then replies, "Tomorrow." He covers his face with his hands so as not to see the bodies rolling into the ravine, and runs along the road, drawn on by an irresistible urge to go forward. He no longer wonders whether he will find a way out. With furrowed brow and clothes in disorder, he runs on in desperation. At last, thinking himself far away from the accursed place, he opens his eyes: there are no more fir-trees; all around are barren stones and grey dust. The sun has disappeared beyond the horizon; night is coming on. The road has lost itself in an endless desert. The desperate traveller, worn out by his long run, wants to stop; but he must walk on. All around him is ruin; he hears stifled cries; his feet stumble on skeletons. In the distance, the thick mist takes on terrifying shapes; black forms loom up; something huge and misshapen suggests itself. The traveller flies rather than walks towards the goal he senses and which seems to flee from him; wild cries direct his steps; he brushes against phantoms.

At last he sees before him a huge edifice, dark, desolate, gloomy, a castle to make one say with a shudder: "A haunted castle." But the young man pays no attention to the bleakness of the place; these great black walls make no impression on him; as he stands on the dusty ground, he hardly trembles at the sight of these formidable towers; he thinks only that the goal is reached, he forgets his weariness and discouragement. As he approaches the castle, he brushes against a wall, and the wall crumbles; instantly everything collapses around him; towers, battlements, walls have vanished, sinking into dust which is added to the dust already covering the ground.

Owls, crows and bats fly out in all directions, screeching and circling around the head of the poor traveller who, dazed, downcast, overwhelmed, stands rooted to the spot, unable to move; suddenly, horror of horrors, he sees rising up before him terrible phantoms who bear the names of Desolation, Despair, Disgust with life, and amidst the ruins he even glimpses Suicide, pallid and dismal above a bottomless gulf. All these malignant spirits surround him, clutch him, propel him towards the yawning chasm. The poor youth tries to resist this irresistible force, he wants to draw back, to flee, to tear himself away from all these invisible arms entwining and clasping him. But it is too late; he moves on towards the fatal abyss. He feels drawn, hypnotized by it. He calls out; no voice answers to his cries. He grasps at the phantoms, everything gives way beneath him. With haggard eyes he scans the void, he calls out, he implores; the macabre laughter of Evil rings out at last.

The traveller is at the edge of the gulf. All his efforts have been in vain. After a supreme struggle he falls... from his bed.

A young student had a long essay to prepare for the following morning. A little tired by his day's work, he had said to himself as he arrived home, "I shall work later." Soon afterwards he thought that if he went to bed early, he could get up early the next morning and quickly finish his task. "Let's go to bed," he said to himself, "I shall work better tomorrow; I shall sleep on it." He did not know how truly he spoke. His sleep was troubled by the terrible nightmare we have described, and his fall awoke him with a start. Thinking over what he had dreamt, he exclaimed, "But it's quite clear: the path is called the path of 'later on', the road is the road of 'tomorrow' and the great building the castle of 'nothing at all'." Elated at his cleverness, he set to work, vowing to himself that he would never put off until tomorrow what he could do today.

1893

6

The Virtues

(A tale for young and old)

Once upon a time there was a splendid palace, in the heart of which lay a secret sanctuary, whose threshold no being had ever crossed. Furthermore, even its outermost galleries were almost inaccessible to mortals, for the palace stood on a very high cloud, and very few, in any age, could find the way to it.

It was the palace of Truth.

One day a festival was held there, not for men but for very different beings, gods and goddesses great and small, who on earth are honoured by the name of Virtues.

The vestibule of the palace was a great hall, where the walls, the floor, the ceiling, luminous in themselves, were resplendent with a myriad glittering fires.

It was the Hall of Intelligence. Near to the ground, the light was very soft and had a beautiful deep sapphire hue, but it became gradually clearer towards the ceiling, from which girandoles of diamonds hung like chandeliers, their myriad facets shooting dazzling rays.

The Virtues came separately, but soon formed congenial groups, full of joy to find themselves for once at least together, for they are usually so widely scattered throughout the world and the worlds, so isolated amid so many alien beings.

Sincerity reigned over the festival. She was dressed in a transparent robe, like clear water, and held in her hand a cube of purest crystal, through which things can be seen as they really are, far different from what they usually seem, for there their image is reflected without distortion.

Near to her, like two faithful guardians, stood Humility, at once respectful and proud, and Courage, lofty-browed, clear-eyed, his lips firm and smiling, with a calm and resolute air.

Close beside Courage, her hand in his, stood a woman, completely veiled, of whom nothing could be seen but her searching

7

eyes, shining through her veils. It was Prudence.

Among them all, coming and going from one to another and yet seeming always to remain near to each one, Charity, at once vigilant and calm, active and yet discrete, left behind her as she passed through the groups a trail of soft white light. The light that she spreads and softens comes to her, through a radiance so subtle that it is invisible to most eyes, from her closest friend, her inseparable companion, her twin sister, Justice.

And around Charity thronged a shining escort, Kindness, Patience, Gentleness, Solicitude, and many others.

All of them are there, or so at least they think.

But then suddenly, at the golden threshold, a newcomer appears.

With great reluctance the guards, set to watch the gates, have agreed to admit her. Never before had they seen her, and there was nothing in her appearance to impress them.

She was indeed very young and slight, and the white dress which she wore was very simple, almost poor. She takes a few steps forward with a shy, embarrassed air. Then, apparently ill at ease to find herself in such a large and brilliant company, she pauses, not knowing towards whom she should go.

After a brief exchange with her companions, Prudence steps forward at their request and goes towards the stranger. Then, after clearing her throat, as people do when they are embarrassed, to give herself a moment to reflect, she turns to her and says:

"We who are gathered here and who all know each other by our names and our merits, are surprised at your coming, for you appear to be a stranger to us, or at least we do not seem to have ever seen you before. Would you be so kind as to tell us who you are ?"

Then the newcomer replied with a sigh:

"Alas ! I am not surprised that·I appear to be a stranger in this palace, for I am so rarely invited anywhere.

"My name is Gratitude."

1904

8

A Sapphire Tale

Once upon a time, far away in the East, there was a small country that lived in order and harmony, where each one in his own place played the part for which he was made, for the greatest good of all.

Farmers, craftsmen, workmen and merchants — all had but one ambition, one concern: to do their work as best they could. This was in their own interest, firstly because, since each one had freely chosen his occupation, it suited his nature and gave him pleasure, and also because they knew that all good work was fairly rewarded, so that they, their wives and their children could lead a quiet and peaceful life, without useless luxury, but with a generous provision for their needs, which was enough to satisfy them.

The artists and scientists, few in number but each devoted to his science or art — his purpose in life — were supported by the grateful nation, which was the first to benefit from their useful discoveries and to enjoy their ennobling works. Thus sheltered from the cares of the struggle for life, these scientists had a single aim: that their experimental research, their sincere and earnest studies should serve to allay the sufferings of humanity, to increase its strength and well-being by making superstition and fear draw back as far as possible before the knowledge that brings solace and enlightenment. The artists, whose whole will was free to concentrate upon their art, had only one desire: to manifest beauty, each according to his own highest conception.

Among them, as friends and guides, were four philosophers, whose entire life was spent in profound study and luminous contemplations, to widen constantly the field of human knowledge and one by one to lift the veils from what is still a mystery.

All were content, for they knew no bitter rivalries and could each devote themselves to the occupation or the study that pleased him. Since they were happy they had no need for many

9

laws, and their Code was only this: a very simple counsel to all, "Be yourself", and for all a single law to be strictly observed, the law of Charity, whose highest part is Justice, the charity which will permit no wastage and which will hinder no one in his free evolution. In this way, very naturally, everyone works at once for himself and for the collectivity.

This orderly and harmonious country was ruled by a king who was king simply because he was the most intelligent and wise, because he alone was capable of fulfilling the needs of all, he alone was both enlightened enough to follow and even to guide the philosophers in their loftiest speculations, and practical enough to watch over the organisation and well-being of his people, whose needs were well known to him.

At the time when our narrative begins, this remarkable ruler had reached a great age — he was more than two hundred years old — and although he still retained all his lucidity and was still full of energy and vigour, he was beginning to think of retirement, a little weary of the heavy responsibilities which he had borne for so many years. He called his young son Meotha to him. The prince was a young man of many and varied accomplishments. He was more handsome than men usually are, his charity was of such perfect equity that it achieved justice, his intelligence shone like a sun and his wisdom was beyond compare; for he had spent part of his youth among workmen and craftsmen to learn by personal experience the needs and requirements of their life, and he had spent the rest of his time alone, or with one of the philosophers as his tutor, in seclusion in the square tower of the palace, in study or contemplative repose.

Meotha bowed respectfully before his father, who seated him at his side and spoke to him in these words:

"My son, I have ruled this country for more than a hundred and seventy years and although, to this day, all men of goodwill have seemed content with my guidance, I fear that my great age will soon no longer allow me to bear so lightly the heavy responsibility of maintaining order and watching over the well-being of all. My son, you are my hope and my joy. Nature has been very generous to you; she has showered you with her gifts and by a wise and model education you have developed them most satisfactorily. The whole nation, from the humblest peasant to our great philosophers, has a complete and affectionate trust in you; you have been able to win their affection by your kindness and their respect by your justice. It is therefore quite natural that their choice should fall on you when I ask for leave to enjoy a well-earned repose. But as you know, according to age-old custom, no one may ascend the throne who is not biune, that is, unless he is united by the bonds of integral affinity with the one who can bring him the peace of equilibrium by a perfect match of tastes and abilities. It was to remind you of this custom that I called you here, and to ask you whether you have met the young woman who is both worthy and willing to unite her life with yours, according to our wish."

"It would be a joy to me, my father, to be able to tell you, 'I have found the one whom my whole being awaits', but, alas, this is yet to be. The most refined maidens in the kingdom are all known to me, and for several of them I feel a sincere liking and a genuine admiration, but not one of them has awakened in me the love which can be the only rightful bond, and I think I can say without being mistaken that in return none of them has conceived a love for me. Since you are so kind as to value my judgment, I will tell you what is in my mind. It seems to me that I should be better fitted to rule our little nation if I were acquainted with the laws and customs of other countries; I wish therefore to travel the world for a year, to observe and to learn. I ask you, my father, to allow me to make this journey, and who knows ? — I may return with my life's companion, the one for whom I can be all happiness and all protection."

"Your wish is wise, my son. Go — and your father's blessing be with you."

11

Amid the western ocean lies a little island valued for its valuable forests.

One radiant summer's day, a young girl is walking slowly in the shade of the wonderful trees. Her name is Liane and she is fair among women; her lithe body sways gracefully beneath light garments, her face, whose delicate skin seems paler for her carmine lips, is crowned with a heavy coil of hair so golden that it shines; and her eyes, like two deep doors opening on limitless blue, light up her features with their intellectual radiance.

Liane is an orphan, alone in life, but her great beauty and rare intelligence have attracted much passionate desire and sincere love. But in a dream she has seen a man, a man who seems, from his garments, to come from a distant land; and the sweet and serious gaze of the stranger has won the heart of the girl — now she can love no other. Since then she has been waiting and hoping; it is to be free to dream of the handsome face seen in the night that she is walking amid the solitude of the lofty woods.

The dazzling sunlight cannot pierce the thick foliage; the silence is hardly broken by the light rustle of the moss beneath the footsteps of the walking girl; all sleeps in the heavy drowse of the noonday heat; and yet she feels a vague unease, as if invisible beings were hiding in the thickets, watchful eyes peeping from behind trees.

Suddenly a bird's song rings out clear and joyful; all uneasiness vanishes. Liane knows that the forest is friendly — if there are beings in the trees, they cannot wish her harm. She is seized by an emotion of great sweetness, all appears beautiful and good to her, and tears come to her eyes. Never has her hope been so ardent at the thought of the beloved stranger; it seems to her that the trees quivering in the breeze, the moss rustling beneath her feet, the bird renewing its melody — all speak to her of the One whom she awaits. At the idea that perhaps she is going to meet him she stops short, trembling, pressing her hands against her beating heart, her eyes closed to savour to the full the exquisite emotion; and now the sensation grows more and more intense until it is so precise that Liane opens her eyes, sure of a presence. Oh, wonder of wonders ! He is there, he, he in truth as she has seen him in her dream... more handsome than men usually are. — It was Meotha.

With a look they have recognised each other; with a look they have told each other of the long waiting and the supreme joy of rediscovery; for they have known each other in a distant past, now they are sure of it.

She places her hand in the hand he offers her, and together, silent in a silence filled with thoughts exchanged, they wend their way through the forest. Before them appears the sea, calm and green beneath a happy sun. A great ship sways gently near the shore.

Meekly, trustingly, Liane follows Meotha into the boat which awaits them, drawn up on the sand. Two strong oarsmen put it to sea and soon bring them alongside the vessel.

Only as she sees the little island disappearing below the horizon does the girl say to her companion:

"I was waiting for you, and now that you have come, I have followed you without question. We are made for each other I feel it, I know it, and I know also that now and forever you will be my happiness and my protection. But I loved my island birthplace with its beautiful forests, and I would like to know to what shore you are taking me."

"I have sought you throughout the world, and now that I have found you, I have taken your hand without asking you anything, for in your eyes I saw that you expected me. From this moment and forever, my beloved shall be all to me; and if I have made her leave her little wooded isle, it is to lead her as a queen to her kingdom, the only land on earth that is in harmony, the only nation that is worthy of Her."

October 1906

13

A Leader

It was in January 1907, shortly after the sangui-
nary crushing of the revolutionary movement in Russia.

A few friends and I had assembled in a small group for
philosophical studies, when we were informed of the presence
of a mysterious visitor asking to be admitted.

We went out to meet him, and in the anteroom we saw a man
whose clean but very worn clothes, arms held close to his sides,
pale face steadfastly turned towards the ground and half-con-
cealed by a black felt hat, made him look like a hunted animal.

At our approach he removed his hat and looked up to cast
us a brief, frank glance.

In the half-light of the hall one could scarcely distinguish the
features of his waxen face; only its sorrowful expression was
clearly visible.

The silence had become embarrassing, and to break it, I
asked, "Can I help you, Sir?"

I have just come from Kiev to see you."

His voice was tired, deep, a little hollow, with a slight
Slavonic accent.

From Kiev to see us! This was something indeed. We were
surprised. He thought our silence indicated doubt, and after
some hesitation he added in a lower tone, "Yes, in Kiev there is
a group of students who are deeply interested in great philosophical ideas. Your books have fallen into our hands, and we
were happy to find at last a synthetical teaching which does not
limit itself to theory, but encourages action. So my comrades,
my friends, told me, 'Go and seek their advice on what is pre-
occupying us.' And I have come."

It was clearly expressed, in correct if not elegant language,
and we immediately knew that if, perhaps out of caution, he
was withholding something from us, what he was telling us at
least was the truth.

14

Once we had brought him in and made him sit down in the drawing-room, we saw him in full light. Oh, the poor face pallid with long vigil or seclusion far from air and sun, ravaged by suffering, lined by anxiety, and yet all shining with a fine intellectual light which haloed his brow and lit his eyes, sad, wan eyes reddened by overwork or perhaps by tears....

Perturbed, we remained silent. But after a while, to find out what he expected of us, we asked him what his occupations were in his own country. He seemed to concentrate, to take some resolve, then slowly said:

"I work for the revolution."

The reply sounded like a knell amid the luxury of this bourgeois apartment.

However, without betraying our emotion, with great admiration for the courage of his sincerity, we replied:

"Would you tell us how we could be of service to you?"

The fact that our attitude towards him had not changed gave him confidence and he began his story:

"You have heard about recent events in Russia, so I will not say anything about that. But perhaps you do not know that at the centre of the revolutionary activity there is a small group of men who call themselves students, to which I belong. Occasionally we meet to take decisions together, but more often we are scattered, firstly so as not to attract attention to ourselves, and secondly to be able to direct the action personally at close quarters. I am their connecting link; when they want to consult together, they meet at my home.

"For a long time we fought openly, violently, hoping to conquer by terror. All means seemed justified to us in our intense and ardent desire to see the cause of Justice, Liberty and Love triumph. You might have seen me, I who feel in my soul a wealth of tenderness and pity that seeks to relieve the miseries of mankind, I who became a doctor with the sole aim of fighting its ills and alleviating its sufferings, being forced by painful circumstances to take the bloodiest decisions. It's surprising,

15

isn't it ? Nobody could have believed that I was suffering because of that; nevertheless, it is a fact. But the others pushed
me, overwhelmed me with good reasons and sometimes succeeded in convincing me.

"However, even in the heat of action, I was aware that there
was something better to do, that our methods were not the best
ones, that we were wasting our finest energies in vain, and that
in spite of the almost fanatical enthusiasm which urged us on,
we might well be defeated.

"The collapse came, mowing us down like corn in a field;
and misfortune compelled us to regain possession of ourselves,
to think carefully. The best of us are lost. The most intelligent,
those who were most able to guide and direct us paid for their
courageous self-sacrifice with exile or death. Consternation
reigned in our ranks; at last I was able to make the others listen
to what I thought, to what I felt.

"We are not strong enough to fight by force, for we are not
united enough, not organised enough. We must develop our
intelligence to understand better the deeper laws of Nature, and
to learn better how to act in an orderly way, to co-ordinate our
efforts. We must teach the people around us, we must train
them to think for themselves and to reflect so that they can
become aware of the precise aim we want to attain and thus
become an effective help to us, instead of being the hindrance
they most often are at the moment.

"I have told them that for a nation to win its freedom, it
must first of all deserve it, make itself worthy of it, prepare itself
to be able to enjoy it. This is not the case in Russia, and we
shall have much to do to educate the masses and pull them out
of their torpor; but the sooner we set to the task, the sooner
we shall be ready for renewed action.

"I have been able to make my friends understand these
things; they trusted me and we began to study. That is how we
came to read your books. And now I have come to ask your
help in adapting your ideas to our present situation and with

them to draw up a plan of action, and also to write a small pamphlet which will become our new weapon and which we shall use to spread these beautiful thoughts of solidarity, harmony, freedom and justice among the people."

He remained thoughtful a moment, then continued in a lower tone·

"And yet I sometimes wonder if my philosophical dream is only a utopia, whether I am wrong to lead my brothers along this path, whether it is only cowardice, in brief, if we would not do better to oppose violence to violence, destruction to destruction, bloodshed to bloodshed, to the very end."

"Violence is never a good way to bring victory to a cause such as yours. How can you hope to win justice with injustice, harmony with hatred ?"

"I know. This opinion is shared by nearly all of us. As for me, I have a very particular aversion to bloody actions; they horrify me. Each time we immolated a new victim, I felt a pang of regret, as if by that very act we were moving away from our goal.

"But what are we to do when we are driven by events and when we are faced with adversaries who will not shrink even from mass slaughter in the hope of overcoming us ? But that they can never do. Though we may perish to the last man, we shall not falter in the sacred task that has fallen to us, we shall not betray the holy cause which we have sworn in our heart of hearts to serve to the last breath."

These few words had been spoken with sombre determination, while the face of this obscure hero was marked with such noble mysticism that I would not have been astonished to see the martyr's crown of thorns encircling his brow.

"But as you were telling us in the beginning," I replied, "since you have yourselves been forced to recognise that this open struggle, this struggle of desperate men, although certainly not without an intrepid greatness, is at the same time vain and foolish in its recklessness, you should renounce it for a time,

17

fade into the shadows, prepare yourselves in silence, gather your strength, form yourselves into groups, become more and more united, so as to conquer on the auspicious day, helped by the organising intelligence, the all-powerful lever which, unlike violence, can never be defeated.

"Put no more weapons in the hands of your adversaries, be irreproachable before them, set them an example of courageous patience, of uprightness and justice; then your triumph will be near at hand, for right will be on your side, integral right, in the means as in the goal."

He had been listening to me carefully, occasionally nodding in agreement. After a silence full of thoughts, in which we could feel brooding around him all the painful hopes, all the burning aspirations of his companions in strife:

"I am happy, Madame," he said, turning towards me, "to see a woman concerned with such matters. Women can do so much to hasten the coming of better days ! There, in Russia, their services have been invaluable to us. Without them we would never have had so much courage, energy and endurance. They move about among us, going from town to town, from group to group, uniting us to one another, comforting the disheartened, cheering the downcast, nursing the sick and everywhere bringing with them, in them, a hope, a confidence, an enthusiasm that never tire.

"So it was that a woman came to assist me in my work, when my eyes were overstrained by my long vigils spent writing by candle-light. For during the day I had to have some kind of occupation so as not to attract attention. It was only at night that I could prepare our plans, compose our propaganda leaflets and make numerous copies of them, draw up lists and do other work of the same kind. Little by little my eyes were burnt up. Now I can hardly see. So a young woman, out of devotion for the cause, became my secretary and writes to my dictation, as long as I wish, without ever showing the slightest trace of fatigue or boredom." And his expression softened and grew tender at the thought of this humble devotion, this proof of self-abnegation.

"She came with me to Paris and we work together every evening. It is thanks to her that I shall be able to write the pamphlet we have spoken of. You know, it is courageous to link one's destiny with a man whose life is as precarious as mine. To retain my freedom, everywhere, I must hide as if I were an outlaw."

"At least you are safe in Paris ?"

"Yes and no. They are scared of us, I don't know why. They take us for dangerous anarchists, and we are watched, we are spied on almost as much as in our own country. Yet how can anyone imagine that men whose aim is to make justice triumph, even at the cost of their own blood, could fail to be grateful towards a country such as France, which has always protected the weak and upheld equity ? And why should they disturb the peace of a city which is their refuge in the darkest days ?"

"So you intend to remain here for some time ?"

"Yes, as long as I can, as long as I am not useful to my brothers there, and can be of service to them here by bringing together all the elements we need to take up the struggle again; but this time the struggle will be as peaceful and intellectual as lies within our power."

"So you will come and see us again, won't you ? Bring us your projects and the plans for your pamphlet. We shall talk about all that again in more detail."

"Yes, I shall come back, as soon as I have started my work, as soon as possible. I shall be so happy to see you again and to continue our conversation."

His kind, sad eyes looked at us full of confidence and hope, while he clasped our hands firmly in his.

And as we accompanied him to the door he turned and once more warmly shook our hands, saying in his grave voice:

"It is good to meet people one can trust, people who have the same ideal of justice as we have and do not look upon

us as criminals or lunatics because we want to realise it.
Good-bye...."

He never returned.

He excused himself in a hastily written note. Too closely
watched, under suspicion, tracked down after he had changed
his lodgings many times, this gentle, just man had to return to
his own country, a terrible country where perhaps a tragic end
awaited him....

To Know How to Suffer

If at any time a deep sorrow, a searing doubt or an intense pain overwhelms you and drives you to despair, there is an infallible way to regain calm and peace.

In the depths of our being there shines a light whose brilliance is equalled only by its purity; a light, a living and conscious portion of a universal godhead who animates and nourishes and illumines Matter, a powerful and unfailing guide for those who are willing to heed his law, a helper full of solace and loving forbearance towards all who aspire to see and hear and obey him. No sincere and lasting aspiration towards him can be in vain; no strong and respectful trust can be disappointed, no expectation ever deceived.

My heart has suffered and lamented, almost breaking beneath a sorrow too heavy, almost sinking beneath a pain too strong.... But I have called to thee, O divine comforter, I have prayed ardently to thee, and the splendour of thy dazzling light has appeared to me and revived me.

As the rays of thy glory penetrated and illumined all my being, I clearly perceived the path to follow, the use that can be made of suffering; I understood that the sorrow that held me in its grip was but a pale reflection of the sorrow of the earth, of this abysm of suffering and anguish.

Only those who have suffered can understand the suffering of others; understand it, commune with it and relieve it. And I understood, O divine comforter, sublime Holocaust, that in order to sustain us in all our troubles, to soothe all our pangs, thou must have known and felt all the sufferings of earth and man, all without exception.

How is it that among those who claim to be thy worshippers, some regard thee as a cruel torturer, as an inexorable judge witnessing the torments that are tolerated by thee or even created by thy own will ?

No, I now perceive that these sufferings come from the very imperfection of Matter which, in its disorder and crudeness, is unfit to manifest thee; and thou art the very first to suffer from it, to bewail it, thou art the first to toil and strive in thy ardent desire to change disorder into order, suffering into happiness, discord into harmony.

Suffering is not something inevitable or even desirable, but when it comes to us, how helpful it can be !

Each time we feel that our heart is breaking, a deeper door opens within us, revealing new horizons, ever richer in hidden treasures, whose golden influx brings once more a new and intenser life to the organism on the brink of destruction.

And when, by these successive descents, we reach the veil that reveals thee as it is lifted, O Lord, who can describe the intensity of Life that penetrates the whole being, the radiance of the Light that floods it, the sublimity of the Love that transforms it for ever !

1910

On Thought

(Talk given to a women's association)

Since we want to learn to think better in order to live better, since we want to know how to think in order to recover our place and status in life as feminine counterparts and to become in fact the helpful, inspiring and balancing elements that we are potentially, it seems indispensable to me that we should first of all enquire into what thought is.

Thought.... It is a very vast subject, the vastest of all, perhaps.... Therefore I do not intend to tell you exactly and completely what it is. But by a process of analysis, we shall try to form as precise an idea of it as it is possible for us to do.

It seems to me that we must first of all distinguish two very different kinds, or I might say qualities, of thought: thoughts in us which are the result, the fruit, as it were, of our sensations, and thoughts which, like living beings, come to us — from where ?... most often we do not know — thoughts that we perceive mentally before they express themselves in our outer being as sensations.

If you have observed yourselves even a little, you must have noticed that the contact with what is not yourselves is established first of all through the medium of your senses: sight, hearing, touch, smell, etc. The impact felt in this way, whether slight or violent, pleasant or unpleasant, arouses a feeling in you — like or dislike, attraction or repulsion — which very quickly turns into an idea, an opinion you form about the object, whatever it may be, that has determined the contact.

An example: you go out and as you step out of your house you see that it is raining and at the same time you feel the damp cold seizing you; the sensation is unpleasant, you feel a dislike for the rain and inwardly, almost mechanically, you say to yourself, "This rain is really a nuisance, especially as I have to go out ! Not to mention that I am going to get dreadfully dirty; Paris is very dirty in rainy weather, especially now that all the streets have been dug up" (and so on)....

All these and many other similar thoughts about the simple fact that it is raining come to assail your mind; and if nothing else, outwardly or inwardly, comes to attract your attention, for a long while, almost without your noticing it, your brain may produce minute, trivial thoughts about this small, insignificant sensation...

This is how most human lives are spent; this is what human beings most often call *thinking* — a mental activity that is almost mechanical, unreflecting, out of our control, a reflex. All thoughts concerning material life and its many needs are of the same quality.

Here we face the first difficulty to be overcome; if we want to be able to truly think, that is, to receive, formulate and form valid and viable thoughts, we must first of all empty our brain of all this vague and unruly mental agitation. And this is certainly not the easiest part of our task. We are dominated by this irrational cerebral activity, we do not dominate it.

Only one method is worth recommending: meditation. But as I was telling you last time, there are many ways of meditating; some are very effective, others less so.

Each one should find his own by successive trial and error. However, one thing can be recommended to everyone: reflection, that is to say, concentration, self-observation in solitude and silence, a close and strict analysis of the multitude of insignificant little thoughts which constantly assail us.

During the few moments you devote each day to this preliminary exercise of meditation, avoid, if possible, the complacent contemplation of your sensations, your feelings, your states of mind.

We all have an inexhaustible fund of self-indulgence, and very often we treat all these little inner movements with the greatest respect and give them an importance which they cer-

24

tainly do not have, even relative to our own evolution.

When one has enough self-control to be able to analyse coldly, to dissect these states of mind, to strip them of their brilliant or painful appearance, so as to perceive them as they are in all their childish insignificance, then one can profitably devote oneself to studying them. But this result can only be achieved gradually, after much reflection in a spirit of complete impartiality. I would like to make a short digression here to put you on your guard against a frequent confusion.

I have just said that we always look upon ourselves with great indulgence, and I think in fact that our defects very often appear to us to be full of charm and that we justify all our weaknesses. But to tell the truth, this is because we lack self-confidence. Does this surprise you ?... Yes, I repeat, we lack confidence, not in what we are at the present moment, not in our ephemeral and ever-changing outer being — this being always finds favour in our eyes — but we lack confidence in what we can become through effort, we have no faith in the integral and profound transformation which will be the work of our true self, of the eternal, the divine who is in all beings, if we surrender like children to its supremely luminous and far-seeing guidance.

So let us not confuse complacency with confidence — and let us return to our subject.

When you are able by methodical and repeated effort to objectivise and keep at a distance all this flood of incoherent thoughts which assail us, you will notice a new phenomenon.

You will observe within yourself certain thoughts that are stronger and more tenacious than others, thoughts concerning social usages, customs, moral rules and even general laws that govern earth and man.

They are your opinions on these subjects or at least those you profess and by which you try to act.

Look at one of these ideas, the one most familiar to you, look at it very carefully, concentrate, reflect in all sincerity, if possible leaving aside all bias, and ask yourself why you have this opinion on that subject rather than any other.

The answer will almost invariably be the same, or nearly:

Because it is the opinion prevalent in your environment, because it is considered good form to have it and therefore saves you from as many clashes, frictions, criticisms as possible.

Or because this was the opinion of your father or mother, the opinion which moulded your childhood.

Or else because this opinion is the normal outcome of the education, religious or otherwise, you received in your youth. This thought is not your own thought.

For, to be your own thought, it would have to form part of a logical synthesis you had elaborated in the course of your existence, either by observation, experience and deduction, or by deep, abstract meditation and contemplation.

This, then, is our second discovery.

Since we have goodwill and endeavour to be integrally sincere, that is, to make our actions conform to our thoughts, we are now convinced that we act according to mental laws we receive from outside, not after having maturely considered and analysed them, not by deliberately and consciously receiving them, but because unconsciously we are subjected to them through atavism, by our upbringing and education, and above all because we are dominated by a collective suggestion which is so powerful, so overwhelming, that very few succeed in avoiding it altogether.

How far we are from the mental individuality we want to acquire !

We are products determined by all our past history, impelled by the blind and arbitrary will of our contemporaries.

It is a pitiful sight.... But let us not be disheartened; the greater the ailment and the more pressing the remedy, the more energetically we must fight back.

The method will always be the same: to reflect and reflect and reflect.

We must take these ideas one after another and analyse them
by appealing to all our common sense, all our reason, our highest sense of equity; we must weigh them in the balance of our
acquired knowledge and accumulated experience, and then endeavour to reconcile them with one another, to establish harmony among them. It will often prove very difficult, for we have
a regrettable tendency to let the most contradictory ideas dwell
side by side in our minds.

We must put all of them in place, bring order into our inner
chamber, and we must do this each day just as we tidy the rooms
of our house. For I suppose that our mentality deserves at least
as much care as our house.

But, once again, for this work to be truly effective, we must
strive to maintain in ourselves our highest, quietest, most sincere state of mind so as to make it our own.

Let us be transparent so that the light within us may fully
illumine the thoughts we want to observe, analyse, classify. Let
us be impartial and courageous so as to rise above our own little
preferences and petty personal conveniences. Let us look at the
thoughts in themselves, for themselves, without bias.

And little by little, if we persevere in our work of classifica-
tion, we shall see order and light take up their abode in our
minds. But we should never forget that this order is but confusion compared with the order that we must realise in the future,
that this light is but darkness compared with the light that we
shall be able to receive after some time.

Life is in perpetual evolution; if we want to have a living
mentality, we must progress unceasingly.

Moreover, this is only a preliminary work. We are still very
far from true thought, which brings us into relation with the
infinite source of knowledge.

These are only exercises for training ourselves gradually to
an individualising control of our thoughts. For control of the
mental activity is indispensable to one who wants to meditate.

I cannot speak to you in detail today about meditation; I

shall only say that in order to be genuine, to serve its full purpose, meditation must be disinterested, impersonal in the integral sense of the word.

Here is a description, taken from an old Hindu text, of a typal meditation:

"The great and magnificent King ascended to the chamber of the Great Collection and, stopping at the threshold, exclaimed with intense emotion:

" 'Away ! Advance no further, thoughts of lust ! Away ! Advance no further, thoughts of bad will ! Away ! Advance no further, thoughts of hate !'

"And entering the chamber, he sat upon a seat of gold. Then, having rejected all passion, all feeling contrary to righteousness, he attained the first *dhāma*, a state of well-being and joy arising from solitude, a state of reflection and seeking.

"Setting aside reflection and seeking, he attained the second *dhāma*, a state of well-being and joy arising from serenity, a state void of reflection and seeking, a state of quietude and elevation of mind.

"Ceasing to delight in joy, he remained indifferent, conscious, self-controlled, and attained the third *dhāma*, experiencing the inmost contentment proclaimed by the sages, saying, 'One who, self-controlled, dwells in indifference, experiences an inner well-being.'

"Setting aside this well-being, rejecting pain, dead to both joy and suffering, he attained the state of most pure and perfect self-mastery and serenity which constitute the fourth *dhāma*.

"Then the great and magnificent King left the chamber of the Great Collection and, entering the golden chamber, sat upon a seat of silver. He beheld the world in a thought of love and his love went forth to the four regions in turn; and then with his heart full of love, with a love growing without end or limit, he enfolded the vast world, in its entirety, to its very ends.

"He beheld the world in a thought of pity and his pity went forth to the four regions in turn; and then with his heart full

28

of pity, with a pity growing without end or limit, he enfolded the vast world, in its entirety, to its very ends.

"He beheld the world in a thought of sympathy and his sympathy went forth to the four regions in turn; and then with his heart full of sympathy, with a sympathy growing without end or limit, he enfolded the vast world, in its entirety, to its very ends.

"He beheld the world in a thought of serenity and his serenity went forth to the four regions in turn; and then with his heart full of serenity, with a serenity growing without end or limit, he enfolded the vast world, in its entirety, to its very ends."[1]

One who strives in sincere quest for truth, who is ready, if necessary, to sacrifice all he had thought until then to be true, in order to draw ever nearer to the integral truth that can be no other than the progressive knowledge of the whole universe in its infinite progression, enters gradually into relation with great masses of deeper, completer and more luminous thoughts.

After much meditation and contemplation, he comes into direct contact with the great universal current of pure intellectual force, and thenceforth no knowledge can be veiled from him.

From that moment serenity — mental peace — is his portion. In all beliefs, in all human knowledge, in all religious teachings, which sometimes appear so contradictory, he perceives the deep truth which nothing can now conceal from his eyes.

Even errors and ignorance no longer disturb him, for, as an unknown master says:

"He who walks in the Truth is not troubled by any error, for he knows that error is the first effort of life towards truth."

But to attain this state of perfect serenity is to attain to the summit of thought.

Without hoping to reach that point at once, we can strive to acquire an individual thought that is both original and as equitable as possible. Thus we shall have become minds of some consequence, with the right to bring to society the precious con-

---

[1] See Appendix page 29.

tribution of their highest intuitions.

I have several times spoken to you this evening of thought as a living and active being. This calls for an explanation. At our next meeting, I shall give you what I might call the chemical or inner structure of thought, its composition, how it is formed, how it lives, acts and transforms.

And now allow me, before concluding, to express a wish.

I would like us to make the resolution to raise ourselves each day, in all sincerity and goodwill, in an ardent aspiration towards the Sun of Truth, towards the Supreme Light, the source and intellectual life of the universe, so that it may pervade us entirely and illumine with its great brilliance our minds and hearts, all our thoughts and our actions.

Then we shall acquire the right and the privilege of following the counsel of the great initiate of the past, who tells us:

"With your hearts overflowing with compassion, go forth into this world torn by pain, be instructors, and wherever the darkness of ignorance rules, there light a torch."

15 December 1911

APPENDIX[1]

LOVE : For the Being, because he is the Being independent of all contingencies and individuals.

PITY : One no longer feels suffering for oneself, but only for others.

SYMPATHY : To suffer with the world, to share suffering (to suffer with).

SERENITY : Perfect knowledge of the state in which all suffering disappears (individual experience).

**

LOVE : For the being in his entirety without distinction of good or evil, light or darkness.

PITY : For all weakness and all bad will.

SYMPATHY : Towards effort, encouragement, collaboration.

SERENITY : Hope in the ending of suffering (knowing one's individual experience, one logically infers that it can be generalised and become the experience of all).

**

LOVE : Without distinction of past, present or future.

PITY : For the life of pain.

SYMPATHY : Understanding of everything, even of evil.

SERENITY : Certitude of the final victory.

**

Three active attitudes, one passive attitude; three external relationships with the all, one inner relationship. A state to be maintained throughout the whole meditation: Serenity in love, sympathy and pity.

---

[1] These notes, found among the Mother's manuscripts, seem to relate to the typal meditation described on pp. 27-28.

On Dreams

At first sight one might think that the subject of dreams is an altogether secondary one; this activity generally seems to have very little importance compared to the activity of our waking state.

However, if we examine the question a little more closely, we shall see that this is not at all the case.

To begin with, we should remember that more than one third of our existence is spent in sleeping and that, consequently, the time devoted to physical sleep well deserves our attention.

I say physical sleep, for it would be wrong to think that our whole being sleeps when our bodies are asleep.

A study based on certain experiments conducted according to the strictest scientific methods, was published some twenty years ago by Dr. Vaschid in a book entitled "Sleep and Dreams".

The doctors who carried out these experiments were led to the conclusion that mental activity never really ceases; and it is this activity which is more or less confusedly transcribed in our brains by what we know as dreams. Thus, whether we are aware of it or not, we always dream.

Certainly, it is possible to suppress this activity completely and to have a total, dreamless sleep; but to be able in this way to immerse our mental being in a repose similar to the repose of our physical being, we must have achieved a perfect control over it, and this is not an easy thing to do.

In most cases, this activity is even heightened, because, as the body is asleep, the internal faculties are no longer focussed on or used by the physical life.

It is sometimes said that in a man's sleep his true nature is revealed.

Indeed, it often happens that the sensory being, which throughout the whole day has been subjected to the control of the active will, reacts all the more violently during the night

32

when this constraint is no longer effective.

All the desires that have been repressed without being dissolved — and this dissociation can only be obtained after much sound and wide-ranging analysis — seek satisfaction while the will is dormant.

And since desires are true dynamic centres of formation, they tend to organise, within and around us, the combination of circumstances that is most favourable to their satisfaction.

In this way the fruit of many efforts made by our conscious thought during the day can be destroyed in a few hours at night.

This is one of the main causes of the resistances which our will for progress often encounters within us, of the difficulties which sometimes appear insurmountable to us and which we are unable to explain, because our goodwill seems so integral to us.

We must therefore learn to know our dreams, and first of all to distinguish between them, for they are very varied in nature and quality. In the course of one night we may often have several dreams which belong to different categories, depending on the depth of our sleep.

As a general rule, each individual has a period of the night that is more favourable for dreams, during which his activity is more fertile, more intellectual, and the mental circumstances of the environment in which he moves are more interesting.

The great majority of dreams have no other value than that of a purely mechanical and uncontrolled activity of the physical brain, in which certain cells continue to function during sleep as generators of sensory images and impressions conforming to the pictures received from outside.

These dreams are nearly always caused by purely physical circumstances — state of health, digestion, position in bed, etc.

With a little self-observation and a few precautions, it is easy to avoid this type of dream, which is as useless as it is tiring, by eliminating its physical causes.

There are also other dreams which are nothing but futile

33

manifestations of the erratic activities of certain mental faculties, which associate ideas, conversations and memories that come together at random.

Such dreams are already more significant, for these erratic activities reveal to us the confusion that prevails in our mental being as soon as it is no longer subject to the control of our will, and show us that this being is still not organised or ordered within us, that it is not mature enough to have an autonomous life.

Almost the same in form to these, but more important in their consequences, are the dreams which I mentioned just now, those which arise from the inner being seeking revenge when it is freed for a moment from the constraint that we impose upon it. These dreams often enable us to perceive tendencies, inclinations, impulses, desires of which we were not conscious so long as our will to realise our ideal kept them concealed in some obscure recess of our being.

You will easily understand that rather than letting them live on unknown to us, it is better to bring them boldly and courageously to the light, so as to force them to leave us for ever.

We should therefore observe our dreams attentively; they are often useful instructors who can give us a powerful help on our way towards self-conquest.

No one knows himself well who does not know the unconfined activities of his nights, and no man can call himself his own master unless he has the perfect consciousness and mastery of the numerous actions he performs during his physical sleep.

But dreams are not merely the malignant informers of our weaknesses or the malicious destroyers of our daily effort for progress.

Although there are dreams which we should contend with or transform, there are others which should on the contrary be cultivated as precious auxiliaries in our work within and around us.

There can be no doubt that from many points of view our subconscient knows more than our habitual consciousness.

Who has not had the experience of a metaphysical, moral or practical problem with which we grapple in vain in the evening, and whose solution, impossible to find then, appears clearly and accurately in the morning on waking ?

The mental enquiry had been going on throughout the period of sleep and the internal faculties, freed from all material activity, were able to concentrate solely on the subject of their interest.

Very often, the work itself remains unconscious; only the result is perceived.

But at other times, by means of a dream, we participate in all the mental activity in its smallest details. Only the cerebral transcription of this activity is often so childish that we normally pay no attention to it.

From this point of view, it is interesting to note that there is nearly always a considerable disparity between what our mental activity is in fact and the way in which we perceive it, and especially the way in which we remain conscious of it. In its own medium, this activity produces vibrations which are transmitted by repercussion to the cellular system of our organic brain, but in our sleeping brain, the subtle vibrations of the suprasensible domain can affect only a very limited number of cells; the inertia of most of the organic supports of the cerebral phenomenon reduces the number of active elements, impoverishes the mental synthesis and makes it unfit to transcribe the activity of the internal states, except into images which are most often vague and inadequate.

To make this disparity more tangible to you, I shall give you an example, one among many, which has come to my knowledge.

Recently, a writer was preoccupied with a half-written chapter which he was unable to finish.

His mind, particularly interested in this work of composition, continued the chapter during the night, and the more it phrased and rephrased the ideas making up the various paragraphs, it became aware that these ideas were not expressed in the most rational order and that the paragraphs had to be rearranged.

All this work was transcribed in the consciousness of our writer in the following dream: he was in his study with several armchairs which he had just brought there and was arranging and rearranging them in the room, until he found the most suitable place for each one.

In the knowledge that certain people may have had of such inadequate transcriptions, we can find the origin of the popular beliefs, the "dream-books" which are the delight of so many simple souls.

But it is easy to understand that this clumsy transcription has a particular form for each individual; each one makes his own distortion.

Consequently, an excessive generalisation of certain interpretations which may have been quite correct for the person applying them to his own case, merely gives rise to vulgar and foolish superstitions.

It is as if the writer we have just mentioned were to impart as a great secret to his friends and acquaintances that every time they saw themselves arranging armchairs in a dream, it was a sign that the next day they would at some moment reverse the order of the paragraphs in a book.

The cerebral transcription of the activities of the night is sometimes warped to such an extent that phenomena are perceived as the opposite of what they really are.

For example, when you have a bad thought against someone and when this bad thought, left to itself, gathers full force during the night, you dream that the person in question is beating you, is doing you some bad turn, or even wounding you or trying to kill you.

Moreover, as a general rule, we should take great intellectual precautions before interpreting a dream, and above all, we should review exhaustively all the subjective explanations before we assign to it the value of an objective reality.

However, especially in those who have unlearnt the habit of always directing their thoughts towards themselves, there are cases where we can observe events outside ourselves, events which are not the reflection of our personal mental constructions. And if we know how to translate into intellectual language the more or less inadequate images into which the brain has translated these events, we can learn many things that our too limited physical faculties do not allow us to perceive.

Some people, by a special culture and training, are even able to become and remain conscious of the deeper activities of their inner being, independently of their own cerebral transcription, and thus to evoke them and know them in the waking state with the full range of their faculties.

Many interesting observations could be made on this topic, but perhaps it is better to allow each one to experience for himself the many possibilities which lie within man's reach in a field of activity which he too often leaves undeveloped.

Uncultivated lands produce weeds. We do not want any weeds in ourselves, so let us cultivate the vast field of our nights.

You must not think that this can be in the least harmful to the depth of your sleep and the efficacy of a repose which is not only indispensable but beneficial. On the contrary, there are many people whose nights are more tiring than their days, for reasons which often elude them; they should become conscious of these reasons so that their will can begin to act on them and remove their effects, that is, to put a stop to these activities which in such cases are nearly always useless and even harmful.

If our night has enabled us to gain some new knowledge — the solution of a problem, a contact of our inner being with some centre of life or light, or even the accomplishment of some useful task — we shall always wake up with a feeling of strength and well-being.

The hours that are wasted in doing nothing good or useful are the most tiring.

But how can we cultivate this field of action, how can we become conscious of our nocturnal activities ?

We shall find the way to do so very broadly outlined in a passage from a book devoted to the study of our inner life :

"The same discipline of concentration which enables man not to remain a stranger to the inner activities of the waking state also provides him with a way to escape from his ignorance of the even richer activities of the various states of sleep.

"These activities usually leave behind them only a few rare and confused memories.

"However, it is noteworthy that a chance circumstance, an impression received, a word pronounced, is sometimes enough to bring suddenly back to the consciousness a whole long dream of which we had no recollection a moment before.

"We can infer from this simple fact that the conscious activity has taken only a very minor part in the phenomena of the sleeping state, since in the normal state of things they would have remained lost for ever in the subconscient memory.

"In this domain, the practice of concentration should therefore focus both on the special faculty of memory and on the participation of the consciousness in the activities of the sleeping state.

"Someone who wishes to recover the memory of a forgotten dream should first of all focus his attention on the vague impressions which the dream may have left behind it and in this way follow its indistinct trace as far as possible.

"This regular exercise will enable him to go further every day towards the obscure retreat of the subconscient where these forgotten phenomena of sleep take refuge, and thus trace out an easily followed path between these two domains of consciousness.

"One useful remark to be made from this point of view is that the absence of memories is very often due to the abruptness of the return to the waking consciousness. (The waking should not be too abrupt.)

"As a matter of fact, at that moment, the new activities

breaking into the field of consciousness force out everything that is unfamiliar to them and add to the difficulty of the subsequent work of concentration needed to recall the things which have been expelled in this way. On the other hand, this work will be made easier whenever certain mental and even physical precautions are observed for a quiet transition from one state to another. (If possible, do not make any abrupt movements in bed at the time of waking.)

"However, this special training of the faculty of memory can only transform into conscious phenomena in the waking state the phenomena which have already been made conscious, even if only fleetingly, during sleep. For where there is no consciousness, there can be no memory.

"Consequently, in the second place, we must work to extend the participation of the consciousness to a greater number of activities in the sleeping state.

"The daily habit of reviewing with interest the various dreams of the night, whose traces will gradually become transformed into precise memories, as well as the habit of noting them down on waking, will be found most helpful from this point of view.

"By these habits, the mental faculties will be led to adapt their mechanism to phenomena of this kind and to exercise on them their attention, their curiosity and power of analysis.

"A kind of intellectualisation of our dreams will then occur, with the double result of making the conscious activities intervene more and more closely in the play of the formerly disorganised activities of the sleeping state, and of progressively increasing their scope by making them more and more rational and instructive.

"Dreams will then take on the nature of precise visions and sometimes of revelations, and useful knowledge of a whole important order of things will be gained."

25 March 1912

The Supreme Discovery

If we want to progress integrally, we must build within our conscious being a strong and pure mental synthesis which can serve us as a protection against temptations from outside, as a landmark to prevent us from going astray, as a beacon to light our way across the moving ocean of life.

Each individual should build up this mental synthesis according to his own tendencies and affinities and aspirations. But if we want it to be truly living and luminous, it must be centred on the idea that is the intellectual representation symbolising That which is at the centre of our being, That which is our life and our light.

This idea, expressed in sublime words, has been taught in various forms by all the great Instructors in all lands and all ages.

The Self of each one and the great universal Self are one.

Since all that is exists from all eternity in its essence and principle, why make a distinction between the being and its origin, between ourselves and what we place at the beginning?

The ancient traditions rightly said:

"Our origin and ourselves, our God and ourselves are one."

And this oneness should not be understood merely as a more or less close and intimate relationship of union, but as a true identity.

Thus, when a man who seeks the Divine attempts to re-ascend by degrees towards the inaccessible, he forgets that all his knowledge and all his intuition cannot take him one step forward in this infinite; neither does he know that what he wants to attain, what he believes to be so far from him, is within him.

For how could he know anything of the origin until he becomes conscious of this origin in himself?

It is by understanding himself, by learning to know himself, that he can make the supreme discovery and cry out in wonder

40

like the patriarch in the Bible, "The house of God is here and I knew it not."

That is why we must express that sublime thought, creatrix of the material worlds, and make known to all the word that fills the heavens and the earth, "I am in all things and all beings."

When all shall know this, the promised day of great transfigurations will be at hand. When in each atom of Matter men shall recognise the indwelling thought of God, when in each living creature they shall perceive some hint of a gesture of God, when each man can see God in his brother, then dawn will break, dispelling the darkness, the falsehood, the ignorance, the error and suffering that weigh upon all Nature. For, "all Nature suffers and laments as she awaits the revelation of the Sons of God."

This indeed is the central thought epitomising all others, the thought which should be ever present to our remembrance as the sun that illumines all life.

That is why I remind you of it today. For if we follow our path bearing this thought in our hearts like the rarest jewel, the most precious treasure, if we allow it to do its work of illumination and transfiguration within us, we shall know that it lives in the centre of all beings and all things, and in it we shall feel the marvellous oneness of the universe.

Then we shall understand the vanity and childishness of our meagre satisfactions, our foolish quarrels, our petty passions, our blind indignations. We shall see the dissolution of our little faults, the crumbling of the last entrenchments of our limited personality and our obtuse egoism. We shall feel ourselves being swept along by this sublime current of true spirituality which will deliver us from our narrow limits and bounds.

The individual Self and the universal Self are one; in every world, in every being, in every thing, in every atom is the Divine Presence, and man's mission is to manifest it.

In order to do that, he must become conscious of this Divine

41

Presence within him. Some individuals must undergo a real apprenticeship in order to achieve this: their egoistic being is too all-absorbing, too rigid, too conservative, and their struggles against it are long and painful. Others, on the contrary, who are more impersonal, more plastic, more spiritualised, come easily into contact with the inexhaustible divine source of their being. But let us not forget that they too should devote themselves daily, constantly, to a methodical effort of adaptation and transformation, so that nothing within them may ever again obscure the radiance of that pure light.

But how greatly the standpoint changes once we attain this deeper consciousness ! How understanding widens, how compassion grows !

On this a sage has said:

"I would like each one of us to come to the point where he perceives the inner God who dwells even in the vilest of human beings; instead of condemning him we would say, 'Arise, O resplendent Being, thou who art ever pure, who knowest neither birth nor death; arise, Almighty One, and manifest thy nature'."

Let us live by this beautiful utterance and we shall see everything around us transformed as if by miracle.

This is the attitude of true, conscious and discerning love, the love which knows how to see behind appearances, understand in spite of words, and which, amid all obstacles, is in constant communion with the depths.

What value have our impulses and our desires, our anguish and our violence, our sufferings and our struggles, all these inner vicissitudes unduly dramatised by our unruly imagination — what value do they have before this great, this sublime and divine love bending over us from the innermost depths of our being, bearing with our weaknesses, rectifying our errors, healing our wounds, bathing our whole being with its regenerating streams ?

For the inner Godhead never imposes herself, she neither demands nor threatens; she offers and gives herself, conceals and forgets herself in the heart of all beings and things; she never accuses, she neither judges nor curses nor condemns, but works unceasingly to perfect without constraint, to mend without reproach, to encourage without impatience, to enrich each one with all the wealth he can receive; she is the mother whose love bears fruit and nourishes, guards and protects, counsels and consoles; because she understands everything, she can endure everything, excuse and pardon everything, hope and prepare for everything; bearing everything within herself, she owns nothing that does not belong to all, and because she reigns over all, she is the servant of all; that is why all, great and small, who want to be kings with her and gods in her, become, like her, not despots but servitors among their brethren.

How beautiful is this humble role of servant, the role of all who have been revealers and heralds of the God who is within all, of the Divine Love that animates all things....

And until we can follow their example and become true servants even as they, let us allow ourselves to be penetrated and transformed by this Divine Love; let us offer Him, without reserve, this marvellous instrument, our physical organism. He shall make it yield its utmost on every plane of activity.

To achieve this total self-consecration, all means are good, all methods have their value. The one thing needful is to persevere in our will to attain this goal. For then everything we study, every action we perform, every human being we meet, all come to bring us an indication, a help, a light to guide us on the path.

Before I close, I shall add a few pages for those who have already made apparently fruitless efforts, for those who have encountered the pitfalls on the way and seen the measure of their weakness, for those who are in danger of losing their self-confidence and courage. These pages, intended to rekindle hope in the hearts of those who suffer, were written by a spiritual worker at a time when ordeals of every kind were sweeping down on him like purifying flames.

You who are weary, downcast and bruised, you who fall, who think perhaps that you are defeated, hear the voice of a friend. He knows your sorrows, he has shared them, he has suffered like you from the ills of the earth; like you he has crossed many deserts under the burden of the day, he has known thirst and hunger, solitude and abandonment, and the cruellest of all wants, the destitution of the heart. Alas ! he has known too the hours of doubt, the errors, the faults, the failings, every weakness.

But he tells you: Courage ! Hearken to the lesson that the rising sun brings to the earth with its first rays each morning. It is a lesson of hope, a message of solace.

You who weep, who suffer and tremble, who dare not expect an end to your ills, an issue to your pangs, behold: there is no night without dawn and the day is about to break when darkness is thickest; there is no mist that the sun does not dispel, no cloud that it does not gild, no tear that it will not dry one day, no storm that is not followed by its shining triumphant bow; there is no snow that it does not melt, nor winter that it does not change into radiant spring.

And for you too, there is no affliction which does not bring its measure of glory, no distress which cannot be transformed into joy, nor defeat into victory, nor downfall into higher ascension, nor solitude into radiating centre of life, nor discord into harmony — sometimes it is a misunderstanding between two minds that compels two hearts to open to mutual communion; lastly, there is no infinite weakness that cannot be changed into strength. And it is even in supreme weakness that almightiness chooses to reveal itself !

Listen, my little child, you who today feel so broken, so fallen perhaps, who have nothing left, nothing to cover your misery and foster your pride: never before have you been so great ! How close to the summits is he who awakens in the depths, for the deeper the abyss, the more the heights reveal themselves !

Do you not know this, that the most sublime forces of the vasts seek to array themselves in the most opaque veils of Matter ? Oh, the sublime nuptials of sovereign love with the obscurest plasticities, of the shadow's yearning with the most royal light !

If ordeal or fault has cast you down, if you have sunk into the nether depths of suffering, do not grieve — for there indeed the divine love and the supreme blessing can reach you ! Because you have passed through the crucible of purifying sorrows, the glorious ascents are yours.

You are in the wilderness: then listen to the voices of the silence. The clamour of flattering words and outer applause has gladdened your ears, but the voices of the silence will gladden your soul and awaken within you the echo of the depths, the chant of divine harmonies !

You are walking in the depths of night: then gather the priceless treasures of the night. In bright-sunshine, the ways of intelligence are lit, but in the white luminosities of the night lie the hidden paths of perfection, the secret of spiritual riches.

You are being stripped of everything: that is the way towards plenitude. When you have nothing left, everything will be given to you. Because for those who are sincere and true, from the worst always comes the best.

Every grain that is sown in the earth produces a thousand. Every wing-beat of sorrow can be a soaring towards glory.

And when the adversary pursues man relentlessly, everything he does to destroy him only makes him greater.

Hear the story of the worlds, look: the great enemy seems to triumph. He casts the beings of light into the night, and the night is filled with stars. He rages against the cosmic working, he assails the integrity of the empire of the sphere, shatters its harmony, divides and subdivides it, scatters its dust to the four winds of infinity, and lo ! the dust is changed into a golden seed, fertilising the infinite and peopling it with worlds which now gravitate around their eternal centre in the larger orbit of space

45

— so that even division creates a richer and deeper unity, and by multiplying the surfaces of the material universe, enlarges the empire that it set out to destroy.

Beautiful indeed was the song of the primordial sphere cradled in the bosom of immensity, but how much more beautiful and triumphant is the symphony of the constellations, the music of the spheres, the immense choir that fills the heavens with an eternal hymn of victory!

Hear again: no state was ever more precarious than that of man when he was separated on earth from his divine origin. Above him stretched the hostile borders of the usurper, and at his horizon's gates watched jailers armed with flaming swords. Then, since he could climb no more to the source of life, the source arose within him; since he could no more receive the light from above, the light shone forth at the very centre of his being; since he could commune no more with the transcendent love, that love offered itself in holocaust and chose each terrestrial being, each human self as its dwelling-place and sanctuary.

That is how, in this despised and desolate but fruitful and blessed Matter, each atom contains a divine thought, each being carries within him the Divine Inhabitant. And if no being in all the universe is as frail as man, neither is any as divine as he!

In truth, in truth, in humiliation lies the cradle of glory!

28 April 1912

PART 2

MEETINGS

In 1912 a small group of seekers met regularly with the aim of gaining self-knowledge and self-mastery.

At the end of each session, a general question was set, which each member was to answer individually. These answers were read out at the next meeting. Then, to close the session, a small essay was read out. Here are the essays.

7 May 1912

What is the most useful work to be done at the present moment ?

The general aim to be attained is the advent of a progressing universal harmony.

The means for attaining this aim, in regard to the earth, is the realisation of human unity through the awakening in all and the manifestation by all of the inner Divinity which is One.

In other words, — to create unity by founding the Kingdom of God which is within us all.

This, therefore, is the most useful work to be done:

(1) For each individually, to be conscious in himself of the Divine Presence and to identify himself with it.

(2) To individualise the states of being that were never till now conscious in man and, by that, to put the earth in connection with one or more of the fountains of universal force that are still sealed to it.

(3) To speak again to the world the eternal word under a new form adapted to its present mentality.

It will be the synthesis of all human knowledge.

(4) Collectively, to establish an ideal society in a propitious spot for the flowering of the new race, the race of the Sons of God.

The terrestrial transformation and harmonisation can be brought about by two processes which, though opposite in appearance, must combine — must act upon each other and complete each other:

(1) Individual transformation, an inner development leading to the union with the Divine Presence.

(2) Social transformation, the establishment of an environment favourable to the flowering and growth of the individual.

Since the environment reacts upon the individual and, on the other hand, the value of the environment depends upon the value of the individual, the two works should proceed side by side. But this can be done only through division of labour, and that necessitates the formation of a group, hierarchised, if possible.

The action of the members of the group should be threefold:

(1) To realise in oneself the ideal to be attained: to become a perfect earthly representative of the first manifestation of the Unthinkable in all its modes, attributes and qualities.

(2) To preach this ideal by word, but, above all, by example, so as to find out all those who are ready to realise it in their turn and to become also announcers of liberation.

(3) To found a typic society or reorganise those that already exist.

*
* *

For each individual also there is a twofold labour to be done, simultaneously, each side of it helping and completing the other:

(1) An inner development, a progressive union with the Divine Light, sole condition in which man can be always in harmony with the great stream of universal life.

(2) An external action which everyone has to choose according to his capacities and personal preferences. He must find his own place, the place which he alone can occupy in the general concert, and he must give himself entirely to it, not forgetting that he is playing only one note in the terrestrial symphony and yet his note is indispensable to the harmony of the whole, and its value depends upon its justness.

14 May 1912

What is my place in the universal work ?

We all have a role to fulfil, a work to accomplish, a place which we alone can occupy.

But since this work is the expression, the outer manifestation of the inmost depth of our being, we can become conscious of its definitive form only when we become conscious of this depth within ourselves.

This is what sometimes happens in cases of true conversion.

The moment we perceive the transfiguring light and give ourselves to it without reserve, we can suddenly and precisely become aware of what we are made for, of the purpose of our existence on earth.

But this enlightenment is exceptional. It is brought about within us by a whole series of efforts and inner attitudes. And one of the essential conditions if we want to achieve and maintain within ourselves these attitudes, these soul-states, is to devote part of our time each day to some impersonal action; every day, we must do something useful for others.

Until we know *the* essential thing we are intended to do, we must therefore find a temporary occupation which will be the best possible manifestation of our present capacities and our goodwill.

Then we shall give ourselves to this occupation with conscientiousness and perseverance, knowing that it may well be only a stage and that with the progress of our ideal and our energies, we shall certainly one day be led to see more clearly the work we must accomplish. To the extent that we lose the habit of referring everything to ourselves and learn more and more to give ourselves more completely, with greater love, to earth and men, we shall see our horizons widen and our duties become more numerous and clear.

We shall find that our action follows a general line of progression determined by our own particular temperament.

Indeed, the successive occupations we shall hold before we become conscious of the definitive form of our action will always point in the same direction, be of the same type and mode, which is the spontaneous expression of our character, our nature, our own characteristic vibration.

The discovery of this tendency, this particular orientation, should come about quite naturally; it is a matter of taste and free choice, beyond all outer selfish considerations.

People are often blamed for choosing an action for themselves which does not correspond to their abilities. There is a slight confusion here.

Those who freely set out to accomplish their own favourite work cannot, in my opinion, be on the wrong track; this work must surely be the expression of their own particular tendency. But their mistake lies in wanting to accomplish this work all at once in its entirety, in its integrality, in depth and above all on the surface, forgetting that the very conception of the work is imperfect as they are imperfect and that to be wise, they should add to the knowledge of what they *wish* to do the more immediate and practical knowledge of what they are *capable* of doing at the present moment.

By taking both these factors into account, they can employ themselves with a minimum waste of time and energy.

But few people act with so much insight and wisdom. And it very often happens that one who is seeking his way falls into one of these two possible errors:

Either he takes his desires for realities, that is, he overestimates his present strength and capacity and imagines that he is capable of immediately assuming a place and a role which he can honourably fulfil only after many years of methodical and persevering effort.

Or he underestimates his latent powers and deliberately confines himself, in spite of his deeper aspirations, to a task which is far beneath his abilities and which will gradually extinguish within him the light that could have shone for others.

It seems difficult at first to steer clear of these pitfalls and find the balanced way, the middle way.

But we have a sure pointer to guide us.

Above all, whatever we undertake should not be done for the purpose of self-assertion. If we are attached to fame and glory, to the esteem of our peers, we are soon led to make concessions to them; and if we seek any opportunity to admire ourselves, it becomes easy to make ourselves out to be what we are not, and nothing more obscures the ideal within us.

We should never tell ourselves, openly or indirectly, "I want to be great, what vocation can I find for myself in order to become great ?"

On the contrary, we should tell ourselves, "There must certainly be something I can do better than anyone else, since each one of us is a special mode of manifestation of the divine power which, in its essence, is one in all. However humble and modest it may be, this is precisely the thing to which I should devote myself, and in order to find it, I shall observe and analyse my tastes, tendencies and preferences, and I shall do it without pride or excessive humility, whatever others may think I shall do it just as I breathe, just as the flower smells sweet, quite simply, quite naturally, because I cannot do otherwise."

As soon as we have abolished within us, even for a moment, all egoistic desires, all personal and selfish aims, we can surrender to this inner spontaneity, this deep inspiration which will enable us to commune with the living and progressive forces of the universe.

The conception of our work will inevitably grow more perfect as we grow more perfect ourselves; and to realise this growing perfection, no effort to exceed ourselves should be neglected, but the work we perform must become always more and more joyful and spontaneous, like water welling from a pure spring.

21 May 1912

> *What is the greatest obstacle in ourselves to our con-*
> *secration to impersonal work ?*

Regarded from the most general point of view, this obstacle is indistinguishable from the very reason for the work to be accomplished: it is the present state of imperfection of physical Matter.

Since we are made up of an imperfect substance, we cannot but share in this imperfection.

Therefore, whatever degree of perfection, consciousness or knowledge is possible to our inmost being, the very fact that it incarnates in a physical body gives rise to obstacles to the purity of its manifestation; and on the other hand, the aim of its incarnation is victory over these obstacles, the transformation of Matter. We must therefore not be surprised or saddened if we encounter obstacles within ourselves, for every single being on earth has difficulties to overcome.

The cause of this imperfection may become apparent to us from two points of view, one general, the other individual.

From the general point of view, the imperfection of Matter comes from its lack of receptivity to the more subtle forces which are to be manifested through it. But this lack of receptivity itself has many causes, and to explain them would lead us too far away from the heart of our subject. Besides, I think that, in the last analysis, all difficulties lie in the illusion of personality, that is, the illusion that one thing can be distinct from the whole.

To avoid speculating on the necessity of this illusion for the very existence of the universe as we know it, I shall consider the question solely from the terrestrial and human angle.

This illusion of a self separate from the whole brings about two tendencies within ourselves.

The first comes from an unconscious need for identification

with the whole. But by the very fact of the illusion of personality, each one conceives this identification only as an absorp-
tion into himself and seeks more or less to be the centre of this
whole. As a result, in proportion to his intellectual or physical
strength, each one attempts to draw to himself everything he is
conscious of in order to continually increase his personality.

This is the outcome of a desire which is justified in essence
— to become conscious of everything — but ignorant in expression, for if a way to become conscious of everything does exist,
it certainly does not lie in trying to draw everything to oneself,
which is absurd and unrealisable, but in identifying one's consciousness with the consciousness of the whole, which demands
the very opposite action and attitude.

The second tendency, which is in fact a normal consequence
of the first, is an excessively conservative spirit, a fixity of the
whole nature — intellectual, moral and physical — which makes
it impossible for us to transform ourselves as rapidly as we
should in order to be always in harmony with the law of universal progress.

It is as if the individual were afraid of not being different
enough from others if he encouraged too free and large an exchange with the whole.

Moreover, this fixity comes from the desire to appropriate
and the error of believing that we can own something in the universe. We think that the elements we are made of are our own.
Consciously or unconsciously, we want to hold on to them for
ourselves while at the same time we are quite ready to add to
them by drawing other elements to ourselves; but we forget that
since there is no real separation, we can receive nothing if we
do not give.

We must be a link in the chain: the link does not grow
bigger at the expense of its neighbours. But when it faithfully
transmits the current it has received, it will receive another, and
the more complete and swift its transmission, the more it will
be brought into contact with a great number of forces or things

for it to use or manifest. And so, little by little, by taking and keeping nothing for itself, it can become aware of everything by communing with everything.

Foreseeing the objections which could be raised, I shall add this:

When I speak of the illusion of personality, I am not denying that each one has a special mode of manifestation. Differentiation does not mean division.

Why should there be so many countless links in the chain if each one did not have its own function ?

And here another comparison is needed to complete the first, for any comparison is necessarily incomplete.

If we consider ourselves as cells of an immense living organism, we shall immediately understand that a cell, which is dependent for its own life on the life of the whole and can separate itself from it only at the risk of destruction, does in fact have its own special part to play in the whole.

But this role is precisely what is most profoundly spontaneous in our being; no egoistic assertion of our personality is needed to discover it. On the contrary, the more fully we give ourselves to an impersonal action, the more this role will gain in strength and clarity within us. But this role is precisely what constitutes our true individuality, since it is our own special way of manifesting the Divine Essence, which is one in everything and in all.

28 May 1912

What is the psychological difficulty which I can best study by experience ?

In each one of us there is a difficulty which is more central than all the others; it is the one which, relative to the part we have to play in the world, is like the shadow of that light, a shadow which gradually dissolves, fades more and more as the light becomes more intense, more brilliant, more powerful and extends to the whole being.

This difficulty, which is particular to each one, seems to me to be the one which deserves all our attention and effort, for if we know how to observe ourselves, we shall see that it is the source of all the others which may obstruct our way.

So this evening, I shall make a brief survey of a difficulty of this kind.

Some people have an excessive sensitivity, which becomes most acute when it does not manifest itself outwardly. This sensitivity is of an affective, emotional kind.

It usually comes from a supra-nervous substance which is highly intellectualised but not spiritualised enough for its degree of intellectualisation.

It is a stage of evolution in which the being is ready for self-giving, for he is conscious of himself; but, as a result of the work of individualisation, of intellectualisation he has undergone, he has acquired the habit of considering everything in relation to himself and has carried the illusion of personality to its utmost limit.

Thus it is sometimes very difficult for him not to watch himself acting, feeling and thinking, and this results in a lack of spontaneity which verges on insincerity.

The being takes pleasure in his extreme sensitivity; he is a delicate instrument which responds marvellously to the least vibration, and so, instead of exteriorising himself and forgetting his own self as he should, he withdraws into himself, observes and analyses and almost contemplates himself.

Thus cultivated, the emotional sensitivity goes on increasing, sharpening and refining itself. And since in life opportunities for suffering are more frequent than opportunities for joy, the need to experience and study these subtle movements of feeling develops an inclination, a taste for suffering, a true mystical aberration which is nothing but self-seeking through suffering, a refined but very pernicious form of egoism.

The practical results of this need to suffer are altogether disastrous if you add to it the intuitive but still inaccurate perception that the work you have to accomplish, your purpose in life, is to draw towards yourself, to take upon yourself, the suffering of others and change it into harmony.

As a matter of fact, on one hand this knowledge is incomplete because you do not know that the only way to relieve others, to eliminate a little suffering in this world, is not to allow any sensitivity, however painful it may seem, to arouse suffering in yourself or to disturb your peace and serenity. On the other hand the idea of the work to be accomplished is itself warped by the illusion of personality. The correct idea is not to draw all suffering to yourself, which is unrealisable, but to identify yourself with all suffering, in all others, to become in it and in them a seed of light and love which will give birth to a deep understanding, to hope, trust and peace.

Until this is well understood, the taste for sacrifice rises in the being; and each time an opportunity for it appears, since you are not *disinterested* in this matter, since you *desire* this sacrifice, it becomes something sentimental and irrational and results in absurd errors which sometimes have disastrous consequences. Even if you are in the habit of reflecting before acting, the reflections preceding the act will necessarily be biased, since they are warped by the taste for suffering, by the desire to have an opportunity to impose a painful sacrifice on yourself.

Thus, consciously or not, instead of sacrificing yourself for the good of others, you sacrifice yourself for the pleasure of it, which is perfectly absurd and of no benefit to anyone.

No action should be deemed good, no action should be undertaken until we know its immediate and, if possible, its distant consequences, and until it appears that they must in the end add, however little, to earthly happiness. But to be able to give a sound judgment on the matter, this judgment must in no way be disturbed by any personal preference, and this implies self-detachment.

Not the detachment which is equivalent to the annihilation of the capacity to feel, but the detachment which brings about the abolition of the capacity to suffer.

By this you should understand that for the time being I am excluding insensitive people, those who do not suffer because the substance they are made of is still too unrefined, too crude to feel, those who are not even ready for suffering.

But of those who have achieved a high development of sensitivity, it can be said that their capacity to suffer is the exact measure of their imperfection.

Indeed, the expression of a true psychic life in the being is peace, a joyful serenity.

Any suffering is therefore a precious indication to us of our weak point, of the point which demands a greater spiritual effort from us.

Thus, to cure in ourselves this attraction for suffering, we must understand the absurdity, the petty egoism of the various causes of our sufferings.

And to cure our excessive and ridiculous desire for sacrifice — too frequently for its own sake, regardless of any useful results — we must understand that if we are to remain in contact with all human sufferings through our sensitivity, we must also be vigilant and discerning enough to dissolve these sufferings as they come; to the clear-sighted, they are purely imaginary.

For, from this point of view, the only way to come to the

help of men is to oppose to their suffering an immutable and smiling serenity which will be the highest human expression of Impersonal Love.

Finally, in a case such as the one I have just shown to you, even more than in any other, it is indispensable to keep in mind that true impersonality does not consist only in forgetting ourselves in our acts, but above all in the fact of not being aware that we are forgetting ourselves.

In short, to be truly impersonal, we must stop noticing that we are being impersonal.

And then the work can be accomplished with a large-hearted spontaneity, in all its perfection.

4 June 1912

What improvements can we bring to our meetings ?

We said one day with regard to the numerous groups that form and disappear almost immediately, that this phenomenon of rapid decay is a result of the conventional and arbitrary factors which enter into the organisation of these groups.

In fact, they are founded upon an ideal prototype originating from one or several minds — a formula which is sometimes very beautiful in theory, but which takes no account of the individuals who with their difficulties and weaknesses must form the living cells of the group.

In my opinion, it is impossible to give an arbitrary form to any being, individual or collective; its form can only be the outer expression which perfectly reflects the quality of its constituent elements.

Because this vital law of formation is not observed, these groups follow one upon another and multiply endlessly; all are fated to the same swift destruction. For instead of being living organisms capable of normal growth, development and expansion, they are nothing but inert conglomerations without any possibility of progress.

We had decided to heed this law and carefully refrain from prematurely deciding upon the conditions of life of our little group. It is not yet born, it has hardly begun its period of gestation. Let us allow it to form and blossom very slowly before making any rules for its existence.

Consequently, it would seem disastrous to me to attempt to organise our meetings according to a preconceived plan or to conform to the ideal of one individual or another or even of all of us. We would then be entering on the way of artificial formations shaped by theory and destined to perish even more rapidly than those institutions which develop according to their own spontaneity, which is the sum total of the varied tendencies of their members.

Certainly, our meetings should progress, since that is the condition of their continuation. But this can only happen if they become an opportunity for each one of us to progress.

For if we want their progress to be sincere and in depth, it must depend on our own.

If we could all bring with us here an ardent aspiration for greater knowledge and wisdom, we would create a contemplative atmosphere, which I would like to be able to call religious, and this atmosphere would be most favourable to our self-perfection.

An atmosphere of spirituality is sometimes a far greater help than an exchange of words; the most beautiful thoughts cannot make us progress unless we have a persistent will to translate them within ourselves into higher feelings, more exact sensations and nobler actions.

Thus, to improve our meetings, the essential condition is our own self-improvement.

If we unify ourselves and identify our consciousness with the consciousness of our Divine Self, our group will become unified. If we enlighten and illumine our intellectual faculties, our group will manifest the light. If we allow impersonal love to permeate our whole being, our group will radiate love. And finally, if we bring order into ourselves, our group will become organised of itself, without our needing to intervene arbitrarily in its formation.

In short, let us become the living cells of the organism we want to bring forth, and let us not forget that on the value of its cells will depend the value of the collective being and its action, its usefulness in the work of universal harmony.

11 June 1912

How can one become master of one's thought ?

First condition. To understand the full importance of this mastery by becoming aware, through observation, that our actions are the exact expression of our thoughts and that so long as we do not have perfect control over our mental activity, these thoughts are nothing but reflexes coming from every outside influence (sensations and suggestions). Thus we do not possess ourselves and can in no way be responsible for ourselves so long as we are not the masters of our thought.

Second condition. To will persistently an effective direction of our mental activity.

Third condition. To observe our thoughts in order to become familiar with them, to know their habitual course and become aware of the ones which have a special affinity with our sensorial and emotional nature.

Fourth condition. To seek in ourselves the idea which seems to be the highest, the noblest, the purest and most disinterested and, until the day we find a more beautiful idea to replace it, to make it the pivot around which our mental synthesis will be built up, the regulating idea in whose light all other thoughts can be seen and judged, that is, accepted or rejected.

Fifth condition. To undergo a regular daily mental discipline. To discover among all the teachings that have been given on this subject the method that seems to be most effective and to follow it scrupulously, rigorously, with energy and perseverance.

Some important recommendations:
To know how to take enough mental rest.
Not to demand from ourselves more than we can do.

To take time into account and to know how to wait patiently for the result of our effort.

Lastly, without neglecting anything we can do ourselves, to know how to rely with childlike trust on the Great Supreme Force, the Divine Force that is One in all beings and all things.

18 June 1912

The Power of Words

It seems unnecessary to draw your attention to the quantity of useless words that are uttered each day; this evil is well known to all, although very few people think of remedying it.

But there are many other words which are spoken needlessly. That is to say, in the course of the day, we often have the opportunity of expressing a helpful wish by pronouncing one word or another, provided that we know how to put the appropriate thought behind the words.

But too often we lose this opportunity of drawing a beneficial mental atmosphere around the people we know and thus of truly helping them. It would be very useful to remedy this neglect.

To do this, we must refuse to allow our minds to remain in that state of vague and passive imprecision which is almost constant in most people.

To cure ourselves progressively of this somnolence, we can, when pronouncing a word, force ourselves to reflect upon its exact meaning, its true import, in order to make it fully effective.

In this regard, we can say that the active power of words comes from three different causes.

The first two lie in the word itself, which has become a battery of forces. The third lies in the fact of living integrally the deep thought expressed by the word when we pronounce it.

Naturally, if these three causes of effectiveness are combined, the power of the word is considerably enhanced.

1) There are certain words whose resonance in the physical world is the perfect vibratory materialisation of the more subtle vibration produced by the thought in its own domain.

If we examine closely this similarity between the vibrations of thought and sound, we can discover the limited number of

6 ·

root syllables which express the most general ideas, and which are to be found in most spoken languages with an almost identical meaning. (This origin of language should not be confused with the origin of written languages, which are of an altogether different nature and correspond to different needs.)

2) There are other words which have been repeated in certain circumstances for hundreds of years and which are instinct with the mental forces of all those who have pronounced them. They are true batteries of energy.

3) Finally, there are words which assume an immediate value when they are pronounced, as a result of the living thought of the one who pronounces them.

To illustrate what I have just said with an example, here is a very powerful word, for it can combine the qualities of all three categories: it is the Sanskrit word "AUM".

It is used in India to express the divine Immanence. There, it is associated with every meditation, every contemplation, every yogic practice.

More than any other sound, this sound "AUM" gives rise to a feeling of peace, of serenity, of eternity.

Moreover, this word is instinct with the mental forces which for centuries all those who have used it have accumulated around the idea that it expresses; and, for Hindus especially, it has the true power of bringing one into contact with the divine Essence it evokes.

And as Orientals have a religious mind and the habit of concentration, few pronounce this word without putting into it the conviction that is needed to make it fully effective.

In China, a similar effect is obtained with a word of identical meaning and somewhat similar sound, the word "TAO".

Our western languages are less expressive; in their present form, they are too far removed from the root language which gave birth to them. But we can always animate a word by the power of our living and active thought.

Besides, there are formulas which we could profitably add

to all those in common use.

These formulas were used in certain ancient schools of initiation. They served as greetings, and in the mouth of one who knew how to think them, they had a very special power of action.

The disciples, the neophytes who were taking their first steps on the path, were greeted: "May the peace of equilibrium be with you."

All those who by their constant and progressive inner and outer attitude had shown their deep and lasting goodwill, were greeted: "May the highest good be yours."

And in certain instructors manifesting especially high forces, this word was endowed with the power of transmitting true gifts, for example, the gift of healing.

67

25 June 1912

What is the most useful idea to spread and what is the best example to set ?

The question can be considered in two ways, a very general one applicable to the whole earth, and another specific one which concerns our present social environment.

From the general point of view, it seems to me that the most useful idea to spread is twofold:

1) Man carries within himself perfect power, perfect wisdom and perfect knowledge, and if he wants to possess them, he must discover them in the depth of his being, by introspection and concentration.

2) These divine qualities are identical at the centre, at the heart of all beings; this implies the essential unity of all, and all the consequences of solidarity and fraternity that follow from it.

The best example to give would be the unalloyed serenity and immutably peaceful happiness which belong to one who knows how to live integrally this thought of the One God in all.

From the point of view of our present environment, here is the idea which, it seems to me, it is most useful to spread:

True progressive evolution, an evolution which can lead man to his rightful happiness, does not lie in any external means, material improvement or social change. Only a deep and inner process of individual self-perfection can make for real progress and completely transform the present state of things, and change suffering and misery into a serene and lasting contentment.

Consequently, the best example is one that shows the first stage of individual self-perfection which makes possible all the rest, the first victory to be won over the egoistic personality: disinterestedness.

At a time when all rush upon money as the means to satisfy

their innumerable cravings, one who remains indifferent to wealth and acts, not for the sake of gain, but solely to follow a disinterested ideal, is probably setting the example which is most useful at present.

2 July 1912

Which minds are nearest to me and what is my ideal work among them ?

Always, in one way or another, life puts in our path those who for some reason are near to us. Each individual creates his own environment according to what he is himself.

And, if such is our dominant preoccupation, all those whom we thus meet on our way are the very ones to whom we can be most useful.

For one who lives constantly in the spiritual consciousness, everything that happens to him takes on a special value and all is conducive to his progressive evolution. It will always be beneficial for him to observe his encounters, to investigate both the apparent and the deeper reasons for them, and, in accordance with his altruistic aspirations, he will ask himself what good he can do in each different case. And according to his own degree of spirituality, his action will always have a greater or lesser spiritualising effect.

If we observe at all attentively the causes which bring us closer to our kind, we see that these contacts occur at various levels of depth in our being, depending on our own special mode of conscious activity.

We can classify these relationships into four main categories corresponding to our four principal modes of activity: physical, vital, psychic and mental. They may have their play in one or several of these categories, simultaneously or successively, according to the quality and type of the manifestation of our activity.

Physical contact is compulsory, so to say, since it depends on the fact that we have a physical body. It inevitably occurs with those who have provided us with this body and with all those who are materially dependent on them. These are the relations of kinship. There are also relationships of proximity: neighbourhood in houses, in the various means of transport, in the street. (I may remark here — and this remark also applies to the other three categories — that this relationship is not necessarily exclusive: this is in fact rare, since we are seldom active on only one plane of our being; what I mean is that the physical relationship is dominant over the other three.)

Vital contact occurs between impulses and desires which are identical or liable to combine in order to complement and heighten one another.

Psychic contact occurs between converging spiritual aspirations.

Mental contact comes from similar or complementary mental capacities and affinities.

Normally, if the predominance of one category is not clearly established — and this can only happen when there is enough order in our being to organise it in all its depth and complexity — we can and should give material help to those who are near to us for physical reasons.

With certain exceptions, material help is the best assistance we can give to the members of our family or to those whom we chance to meet in the street, in trains, in ships, in buses, etc.: pecuniary help, aid in case of illness or danger.

We should assist the sensitivity of those who are attracted to us because they have identical tastes, artistic or otherwise, by rectifying, balancing or canalising their sense-energies.

We can help those who by a common aspiration for progress have been brought into contact with us, through our example, by showing them the path, and through our love, by smoothing the way for them.

Finally, we must allow the light of our intelligence to shine for those who come close to us as a result of mental affinity, so that, if possible, we may widen their field of thought and enlighten their ideal.

These various affinities express themselves outwardly in slight and sometimes subtle variations in the conditions of our encounters, and because our insight is seldom alert enough, these slight variations often elude us.

But to direct our action in the right way and reduce as far as possible the causes of our wrong attitudes towards our fellowmen, we should always investigate with the greatest care the numerous reasons for our contacts and find the category of affinities which binds us to them.

A few rare beings are close to us in all four modes of existence at the same time. These are friends in the deepest sense of the word. It is on them that our actions can have their most integral, their most perfectly helpful and beneficial effect.

We should never forget that the duration of a contact between two human lives depends on the number and depth of the states of being in which the affinities that bind them have their play.

Only those who commune with the eternal essence within themselves and in all things can be eternally united.

Only those are friends forever who have been close or distant friends from all time in this or other worlds.

And whether or not we meet these friends depends on the encounter we must first experience within ourselves, in the unknown depths of our being.

Moreover, when this meeting occurs, our whole attitude is transformed.

When we become one with the inner Godhead, we become one in depth with all, and it is through Her and by Her that we must come into contact with all beings. Then, free from all attraction and repulsion, all likes and dislikes, we are close to what is close to Her and far from what is far from Her.

Thus we learn that in the midst of others we should become always more and more a divine example of integral activity both intellectual and spiritual, an opportunity which is offered to them to understand and enter upon the path of divine life.

PART 3

Between 1911 and 1913 the Mother gave a number of talks to different groups in Paris. Two of them, "On Thought" and "On Dreams", appear in Part 1. The same talk was sometimes presented to two or more groups with suitable variations. Additions and alternative versions have been given here as footnotes.

On Thought - II

You probably remember that, last month, we made two observations.

The first is that thought is a living, active, autonomous entity.

The second is that in order to contend victoriously with the injurious effects of the polluted mental atmosphere in which we live, we must build up within ourselves a pure, luminous and powerful intellectual synthesis.

For this purpose we must bring down into ourselves the highest thoughts within our reach, that is, within the field of our mental activity, and make them our own.

But since thoughts are living beings, they have, as we do, their likes and dislikes, their attractions and repulsions.

We must therefore adopt a special attitude towards them, treat them as people, make advances and concessions to them and show them the same attentions as we would to someone we would wish to be our friend.

On this matter, a modern philosopher writes:

"Sometimes thinkers in their meditations, explorers and prospectors of the intellectual world in their discoveries, and poets — the diviners of thought — in their dreams, feel and vaguely sense that the idea is not something abstract and bodiless. It appears to them to be winged, something which soars, comes close and flees, denies and gives itself, something which must be called, pursued and won.

"To the most clairvoyant, the idea seems to be an aloof person with her whims and desires, her preferences, her queenly disdain, her virgin modesty. They know that it takes much care to win her and but a little thing to lose her, that there is a love of the mind for the idea, a love made of consecration and sacrifice, and without this the idea cannot belong to it.

"But these are pretty symbols, and few indeed can perceive the very precise reality which lies beneath them.

75

"It needed a Plato to identify this thing which lives and vibrates, which moves and shines, travels and is propagated through time and space, which acts and wills and freely chooses its own time and place — in short, to know the Idea as a being."

Let us take especially one phrase from this beautiful page : "There is a love of the mind for the idea, a love made of consecration and sacrifice, and without this the idea cannot belong to it."

This is not an image. To enter into an intimate and conscious relation with the idea, we must consecrate ourselves to it, love it with a disinterested love, in itself, for itself.

Today we shall try to find out what this love consists of and, at the same time, what we must do for it to blossom within us.

The first attitude to be taken, the most indispensable, is the most perfect mental sincerity it is within our power to acquire.

Of all sincerities, this is perhaps the most difficult. Not to deceive oneself mentally is not an easy thing to achieve.

First of all we have, as I explained to you last December, a certain habit of thought which comes from the education we have received, from the influence of the environment, and which is most often made up of social conventions and collective suggestions. This habit naturally makes us give a far better reception to all the thoughts which are similar, if not conformable, to those which already fill our minds, than to those which could, to however small an extent, unsettle this mental structure.

For the same reason, as you probably remember, it is sometimes so difficult for us to learn to think for ourselves: we hesitate to change anything whatsoever in our customary way of thinking, which is most often made up of social conventions and collective suggestions. For our whole existence is based upon this habit. It takes a great courage and a great love of progress to consent to examine one's existence in the light of thoughts that are deeper, and consequently more independent of the customs and usages of the environment.

You can judge from this the great, the very great love of the idea that is needed to achieve such a revolution in one's habits, for the sole purpose of gaining the power to enter into a more intimate, more conscious relationship with it !

And even when our mental synthesis is made up of thoughts that we have received and made our own in the course of a constant and persevering effort of meditation, we must love the idea with a very powerful love, perhaps even more powerful still, so that we may always be in quest of a new idea, ready to give it the most eager reception if it is willing to come to us. For we are well aware that each new idea will constrain us to modify our synthesis, relegate to the background ideas which had seemed to us master-ideas, bring to the light other ideas too long disregarded, rearrange them all so that they do not clash, to the great detriment of our brain, in brief, a long and sometimes painful task. Indeed we are very seldom disinterested with regard to ideas; there are some which we prefer to others and which, consequently, occupy a place in our mental activity which they do not always deserve.

And if we must replace them with others that are more precise, more true, we often hesitate long before doing so, we cling to them as indispensable friends, and we love their defects as well as their qualities, — which is the worst way to love people, as well as the laziest and most selfish, — for we are always more highly esteemed by those we flatter than by those from whom we demand a constant effort of progress. But our difficulties do not stop there.

As a consequence of the intellectual education we have received or of some personal preference, we are also prejudiced about the way, or ways, in which ideas should be introduced to us.

These preconceptions are so many veritable superstitions that we must overcome.

They are different for each person.

Some people have the superstition of the book. For an idea

to merit consideration in their eyes, it must have been expressed in some famous book, in one of the bibles of humanity, and any thought coming in any other way will appear suspect to them.

There are some who accept an idea only from the official sciences, and those who recognise one only in the established religions, old or new. For others, the idea must come from the mouth of a man of renown with enough honorary titles so that none can question his value.

Still others, more sentimental, in order to come into contact with thought, need a master who should be the perfect incarnation of the ideal human standard constructed by their imagination. But they are bound to be sorely disappointed, for they forget that they alone are capable of realising their own ideal, that the one in whom they have placed their confidence has a duty to realise his own ideal which, consequently, however great it may be, may very well differ considerably from their own. So, most often, when they become aware of these divergences, since they had attached themselves to the ideas only for the sake of the man, they will reject both man and ideas together.

This is absurd, for ideas are worth what they are worth regardless of the individuals who have expressed them.

Finally, there is a whole category of people enamoured of the miraculous, who will recognise a truth only if it has come to them clothed in the mystery of a supramundane revelation, in dream or trance.

For them the master must be their God, an angel or a Mahatma, and give them his precious teachings during their contemplation or their sleep.

Needless to say, this method is still more unreliable than the others. That a thought should reach us by extraordinary means is no guarantee of its correctness or its truth.[1]

You see, the true lover of the idea knows that by seeking

---

[1] *Paragraph added when this talk was presented to a different group:*

I do not mean that it is impossible to come into contact with an idea by these means, but they are far from being the only ones or even perhaps the best.

78

it ardently he will find it everywhere, and even more so in the subterranean and secret fountainheads than in those which have lost their pristine purity by turning into rivers that are majestic and renowned but also polluted by the waste of all kinds which they carry with them.

The lover of the idea knows that it can come to him from the mouth of a child as from the mouth of a learned man.

And it is even in this unexpected way that it can reach him most often.

That is why it is said : "Out of the mouths of babes and sucklings comes forth truth."

For if the thought of a child cannot have the precision of the thought of a man, neither does it have the fixity which results from laziness of habit and which in the adult prevents the thought from expressing itself whenever it does not belong to the categories which are familiar to him.

Moreover, it was to escape the distortion of an environment made up of habit and fixity that the schools of ancient times where the young prophets were educated were established far from the cities.

That is also why the great instructors of men began their apprenticeship in solitude. For if too many things are absent for the thought to be able to express itself in the minds of unrefined men, too many things are also absent from the mind of the cultivated man shaped by the artificial life of human societies.

How much silence is needed — not the outer, illusory and momentary silence, but on the contrary the true, profound, integral, permanent silence — to be able to hear the far-off voices of thought !

That is why the sincere lover of knowledge also knows that the greatest sages are always the most modest and the most unknown. For one who has the knowledge and the capacity prefers silence and retirement where he is free to accomplish his work without being disturbed by anything, to the fanfares of glory which would throw him as fodder to men.

The lover of thought knows that he will find thought everywhere around him, in the little flower as in the radiant sun; nothing and no one appears to him too humble or too obscure to be for him an intermediary of the idea he is ever seeking.

But above all he knows that the best, the most reliable contact with the idea is certainly a direct contact.

Since we are made out of the universal substance, we are this universe in miniature.

Since no phenomenon can exist without a corresponding medium, the existence of ideas implies the existence of a corresponding domain, the realm of free intelligence always in form but not subject to form, and this realm is within us as within the great universe.

If then we concentrate sufficiently, if we become conscious of our inmost being, we shall come into contact, within it and through it, with the free universal intelligence, the world of ideas.

Then, if we have taken care to polish our mirror well and to clear it of all the dust of preconception and habit, all ideas will be able to reflect themselves there with a minimum of distortion, and we shall have acquired bodhi (knowledge), we shall have acquired the power of reflecting the rays of the Sun of Truth[1] — such was the hope which Siddhartha Gautama held out to us. When he was asked, "How shall we obtain bodhi ?", he would reply:

"Bodhi has no distinctive signs or marks: what can be known in respect of it is of no use whatsoever; but the care we take in practising its spirit is of great importance. It is like a

---

[1] *In a version presented to another group the paragraph ends here and is followed by these two paragraphs:*

Then will our mental actions take on their full power and effectivity. Our thought-formations will become useful and luminous messengers going forth to do their work of goodness and harmony wherever material circumstances prevent us from doing it physically.

And by a little effort of concentration we shall rapidly succeed in becoming conscious of these actions while at the same time remaining in touch with the emanated thought.

cleansed and polished mirror that has become clear and bright, so that images are reflected in it sharply and vividly."

And again:

"One who is without darkness, free from blemish, of blameless conduct, perfectly pure, that one, even though he does not know and has never heard and in short has no knowledge, however little, of any of the things that are in the world of the ten regions since time without beginning until today, none the less, he possesses the highest knowledge of the one who knows all. He is the one of whom it is said: Clarity." You see here a panegyric of the direct relationship with the idea as opposed to the wholly external and superficial method of erudition.

The advantages of this direct relationship are incalculable.

It enables us to recover and love the idea behind all appearances, all veils, all forms, even the most barbarous, the most crude, the most superstitious.

Thus we can put into living practice the state of mind of the sage, of which I spoke to you in my first talk and which a master defines in this way:

"One who advances in Truth is not troubled by any error, for he knows that error is the first effort of life towards truth."

Consequently, not a single fragment of an idea can ever be lost for us; wherever it is concealed, we know how to discover and cherish it.

Moreover, when we have become familiar with an idea, when we know it in itself, for itself, we recognise it behind the most diverse appearances, the most varied forms.

This faculty can even serve as a criterion to discover whether someone is in contact with the idea itself, that is to say, whether he has understood it well and made it his own or whether he is part of the mass of those who have assimilated as best they could a doctrine, a special language, and who can think only in the words of that language — outside this formula, they no longer understand anything.

This attachment to form, which consists entirely of intel-

81

lectual impotence, is one of the most powerful causes of dissension among men.

But one who penetrates deeply enough to see the thought, the naked truth, soon realises that it is the same behind its varied and more or less opaque veils.

This is the surest way to achieve true tolerance.

Indeed, how can we have an exclusive passion for one particular doctrine or school or religion when we have had the experience that each one of them contains treasures of light and truth, however varied the caskets which enclose them ?

16 February 1912

On Thought - III

It has always seemed to me that apart from a very few exceptions, the mental role of women is not to speculate on the metaphysical causes of the phenomena which are perceptible to us, but to draw practical conclusions from these phenomena.

Madame Martial was telling you very rightly last Friday that it would be wrong for women to want to think in the same way as men, that they would be in danger of losing their own qualities — profound intuition and practical deduction — without acquiring those of their masculine counterparts — logical reasoning and the capacity of analysis and synthesis.

That is why today I shall not attempt to demonstrate to you by logical reasoning and transcendental speculation that thoughts exist as true, autonomous, living and active entities.

Besides, if we do not want to indulge in idle talk, if, very sincerely, we want to explain the smallest phenomenon, we must always go back to the most universal general laws. The whole universe is necessary to explain a grain of sand. And this is not the programme we have chosen for the *Union de Pensée Féminine*. Those who, as a result of the teaching they have received and the cerebral gymnastics they have undertaken, are fond of taking up vast metaphysical problems, will find an excellent opportunity to do so at the *École de la Pensée* on the first Friday of each month.[1]

At the *Union de Pensée Féminine*, we shall be more modest, if you agree.

Women, by their very nature, are more capable of taking

---

[1] *Alternative version intended for another group:*

I do not know if you are familiar with the notion of thought as a living and autonomous entity. I shall not venture here to prove its exactitude to you, and this for two reasons.

The first is that in order to explain the smallest phenomenon (for such is our usual way of proving its reality to ourselves), it is necessary to bring in the most universal general laws. Many times we have been led to observe that the whole universe is necessary to explain a grain of sand. And this

83

the spiritual or, in the deepest sense of the word, moral stand-point.

We are essentially realistic and formative in this spiritual domain; we want to know how to live well, and for this we must learn how to think well.

To realise the primary importance of thought, we must know it as it is, that is, as a living being; and so that you may be convinced of the autonomous existence of thought, I shall ask you only to ascertain this for yourselves, which is an easy thing to do.

A little observation will enable us to realise that very often, for example, we receive thoughts which come to us from outside, although we have not been brought into contact with them either by speech or reading.

Who has not also observed this phenomenon: a thought which is "in the air", as we say, and which several inventors, several scientists, several literary men receive simultaneously without having been in physical communication on this matter ?

One could go on giving examples indefinitely. I leave each one to reflect and find the examples which seem most conclusive to her.

Before proceeding further with our subject I shall read you a page on thought which may help you to understand it.

It is a page from an as yet unpublished philosophical volume.

"Any phenomenon implies a corresponding substance; any

---

enquiry would lead us really too far tonight.

On the other hand, to do this, we would have to devote ourselves to lengthy metaphysical speculations, and there is nothing I dread more than this form of mental activity.

Faithful in this matter to the teaching of the Buddha, I am convinced that we can make a far better use of our time and minds than in hazardous excursions into the intellectual realm which, in the last analysis, always eludes our enquiry and inevitably brings us face to face with the unthinkable.

The Buddha always categorically refused to answer any metaphysical question on the origin or the end of the universe, saying that only one thing matters: to advance on the Way, that is, to purify oneself inwardly, to destroy in oneself all egoistic desire.

vibration necessitates a medium of its own; and if vibrations of light require the medium which we know as ether, will not a medium be needed for the more subtle, more mysterious and also more rapid vibrations of thought ?

"I am not speaking of a thought which has already assumed the form and substance provided by the materiality of the brain. Psychologists know very well that before it attains to its modes of conscious activity there, a thought must first of all have passed through remoter states, through the unknown regions of what we call the subconscient.

"It has come from the inner depths to our surface self like a meteor reaching us from inaccessible spaces.

"What was the origin of this meteor, the source of this thought ? We do not know, but they exist, the one beyond our sun, the other probably beyond light.

"There is a relationship of ascendance between light and thought. To go from one to the other in the scale of imponderables, it is necessary to mount a step: conceiving (*concevoir*) is a higher way of seeing (*voir*).

"If we do not see thought, it is because its substance is more ethereal than that of light; just as, if we do not hear light, it is because its essence is more subtle than that of sound.

"Among the elements of its own order, thought moves just as our bodies do among physical objects. Just as our hands know how to shape these objects, in the same way thought also knows how to mould these elements and cast them into a myriad appropriate forms.

"Thus our intellectual gestures are no less fruitful than our physical gestures. And that is why wisdom has always taught that we must watch over our thoughts as we would over generating acts."

So we see that thought, which is a dynamism in the highest sense of the word, acts in its own realm as a formative power in order to build a body for itself. It acts like a magnet on iron filings. It attracts all the elements which are akin to its own character, aim and tendencies, and it vivifies these elements — which are the constituent cells of its own body, that I shall call fluidic to avoid going into too many explanations — it animates them, moulds them, gives them the form which is best suited to its own nature.

We shall find a striking analogy between the work of thought and the work of the inventor, the builder of any kind.

Let us take as an example a steam engine. The engineer draws up a plan in its smallest details, calculates and arranges everything, then he selects the appropriate materials for the materialisation of his conception, watches over the construction, etc.

And when the engine works, becoming by its movement a real living being, it will be the most complete possible manifestation of the thought which has built it, it will give the full measure of the power of this thought. (The awakened unconsciousness of locomotives, cars, ships.) The formative thought, a living entity, animates the body which has been built for it by the hands of men. In the mental domain also, there are conscious builders.

There are people who are specially gifted or who have developed certain inner senses in themselves, who can come into direct contact with this domain, mainly through vision and touch.

When they are thus able to watch over the working of the phenomenon, they can, like chemists in their laboratories, manipulate substances, select them, mould them by their will-power and clothe their thoughts in forms that can manifest them fully.

But this is the ultimate stage of one of the many paths of individual progress. Long before achieving this full consciousness, it is possible to make powerful formations. Any person whose thought has any strength and persistence is constantly making formations without being aware of it.

If you keep in mind that these formations are living entities always acting in the direction imparted to them by the thoughts which have given them birth, you will easily perceive the considerable consequences of these mental acts.

Just as a good, kind, just and lofty thought can be eminently beneficial, so also a malevolent, base, wicked and selfish thought can be baneful.

On this matter, I shall quote to you a passage from the Dhammapada which will give you an idea of the enormous importance attributed to thought by the wisdom of the past.

"Whatever an enemy may do to an enemy, whatever a hater may do to a hater, the harm caused by a misdirected thought is even greater still.

"Neither father nor mother nor any other kinsman can do so much good as a well-directed thought."

If you reflect upon the incalculable number of thoughts which are emitted each day, you will see rising before your imagination a complex, mobile, quivering and terrible scene in which all these formations intercross and collide, battle, succumb and triumph in a vibratory movement which is so rapid that we can hardly picture it to ourselves.

Now you realise what the mental atmosphere of a city like Paris can be, where millions of individuals are thinking — and what thoughts ! You can picture this teeming, mobile mass, this inextricable tangle. Well, in spite of all the contradictory tendencies, wills and opinions, a kind of unification or identity gets established among all these vibrations, for all of them — with a few minor exceptions — all express craving, craving in all its forms, all its aspects, on all planes.

All the thoughts of worldly-minded people whose only aim is enjoyment and physical diversion, express craving.

All the thoughts of intellectual creators or artists thirsting for esteem, fame and honour, express craving.

All the thoughts of the ruling class and the officials hankering after more power and influence, express craving.

All the thoughts of the thousands of employees and workmen, of all the oppressed, the unfortunate, the downtrodden struggling for some improvement of their cheerless existence, express craving.

All, rich or poor, powerful or weak, privileged or deprived, intellectual or obtuse, learned or ignorant, all want gold, always more gold to satisfy all their cravings.

If from place to place there occasionally flashes out a spark of pure and disinterested thought, of will to do well, of sincere seeking for truth, it is very soon swallowed up by this material flood that rolls like a sea of slime....

And yet we must kindle the stars that one by one will come to illumine this night.

But for the moment we are living within it, soaking it up, for in the mental as in the physical domain we are in a state of perpetual interchange with the environment.

This is to point out to you how we are contaminated each day, at each minute.

Can any one of us say that she has never felt craving and that she will never feel it again ? Besides, how could we not feel craving when the atmosphere we breathe is saturated with it ? How could we not feel this host of desires rising in ourselves when all the vibrations we receive are made of desires ?...

And yet if we want our thought to be beneficial and effective we must free ourselves of this bondage.

With this fact in mind, let us first of all draw a practical conclusion: let us be lenient towards all, for temptation is strong and human ignorance is great indeed.

But just as we must be compassionate and kind to others, we must be exacting and strict with ourselves, since we want to become lights in the darkness, torches in the night.

We must therefore learn to resist this daily pollution victoriously.

The very fact of knowing that there is a danger of contagion is already a great step towards liberation. But it is far from sufficient.

There are two possible victories to be won, one collective, the other individual. The first is, so to say, positive and active, the second negative and passive.

To win the positive victory it is necessary to declare an open war of idea against idea, for the thoughts that are disinterested, lofty and noble to give battle to those that are selfish, base and vulgar. This is a real hand-to-hand fight, a struggle of each minute which demands considerable mental power and clarity. For to fight against thoughts it is first of all necessary to receive them, to admit them into oneself, deliberately allow oneself to be contaminated, absorb the sickness into oneself the better to destroy the deadly germ by healing oneself. It is a real war in which one imperils one's mental balance at every minute — and a war demands warriors. I shall not recommend this practice to anyone. It belongs by right to the initiates who have prepared themselves for it by long and rigorous discipline, and we shall leave it to them.

For our part, we shall be content to asepticise ourselves so as to be safe from all infection. We shall aspire therefore for the individual victory, and if we win it we shall find out that we have done more for the collectivity in this way than we suspected at first.

To win this victory we must build up in ourselves a mentality whose quality is the opposite of that of the surrounding medium. We must, little by little, day by day, fill our minds with the loftiest, purest, most disinterested thoughts we can conceive of and by our deliberate care they must become sufficiently alive so that they may awaken within us each time a temptation to think wrongly comes to us from outside, so that they may rise in their dazzling splendour to face the shadow which constantly lurks in wait ready to assail us.

Let us light within ourselves the fire of the ancient vestals, the fire symbolising divine intelligence, which it is our duty to manifest.

This work cannot be achieved in a day or a month or even

89

a year. We must will, and will with perseverance. But if you could know the benefits one reaps from this, if you could feel that peace, that perfect serenity which gradually replaces in us the agitation, the anxiety and fear which spring from desire, you would unhesitatingly set to work.

Moreover, the building up of a synthesis of pure and powerful thoughts does not lead solely to our own happiness. The clearer and higher the flame, the more light it sheds around it.

The star we allow to shine through us will foster the birth of similar stars by its example; fortunately, not only darkness and ignorance, but also knowledge and light can be contagious.

In addition, the care we take to remain conscious of our highest thoughts will compel us to control our thoughts constantly, and this control is gradually obtained by the methods I outlined to you last month — analysis, reflection, meditation, etc. Those who have achieved the control of their mental being can emanate at will a certain portion of their intellectual power, send it wherever they think proper, while remaining perfectly conscious of it.

These emanations, which are true messengers, will take your place wherever, physically, it is for any reason impossible for you to go yourself.

The advantages of this power will be easily apparent to you.

A thought which is skilfully directed and sustained can, by affinity, awaken to consciousness a glimmer of wisdom in many minds as yet wrapt in darkness, and thus set them on their way towards progressive evolution; it can serve as an intermediary for one who is sick by drawing towards him the vital forces needed to cure him; it can watch over a dear friend and protect him from many dangers, either by warning him through mental communication and through his intuition or by acting directly on the cause of peril.

Unfortunately, the inverse is also true, and bad thoughts as well are not wanting in power of action.

We cannot imagine all the harm we do by receiving and emanating bad thoughts, thoughts of hate, vengeance, jealousy, envy, malevolent thoughts, harsh judgments, sectarian valuations....

We all know how injurious it is to listen to and repeat slanderous gossip, but it is not enough to abstain from the words, we must also abstain from the thoughts.[1]

Besides, a little reflection will suffice for this, for we shall very soon understand how rash our judgments and estimations always are.

With regard to acts, to actions committed, we shall be able to tell ourselves again and again that we do not know them exactly as they are, that in any case, the motives behind these acts, the many causes which have determined them, almost completely elude us.

With regard to defects, let us not forget that those which annoy us most in others are usually those which thrive most in ourselves and that, in any case, if we did not have any seeds of these defects within us, we would not be able to perceive them anywhere. Besides, what exactly is a defect? Most often it is the reverse side of a quality, an excess of virtue which has found no outlet, something which is not in its place.

As for what concerns us personally, we must be more prudent still and follow one strict rule very scrupulously: never judge anything without first having put ourselves in the place of the other, whoever he may be, with the greatest possible impersonality; try to feel what he has felt, see what he has seen, and

[1] *Passage added when presented to another group:*

For nothing is more pernicious to ourselves and to others than this uncharitable state of mind. How many times we have felt a kind of unsurmountable barrier rising up between ourselves and someone we know. And yet, towards this person, our words and acts have always been perfectly courteous and occasionally even very friendly.

But where this person is concerned, within ourselves, we have given rein to this spirit of analysis and criticism which lightly dismisses good qualities and fastens only on shortcomings, no doubt without any spitefulness, but with a shade of irony or malice, a feeling of our own superiority — wretched as we are! And so, little by little, drop by drop, between this person and ourselves, a veritable river is formed which separates us more and more from each other, despite whatever physical efforts we may make to come closer together.

91

if we succeed in being perfctly sincere, very often we shall see our estimation becoming less strict and more just.

Besides, as a general rule, in what light shall we look at what we want to judge ? What shall our criterion be ? Indeed, do we fancy that we possess the supreme wisdom and the perfect justice that we are able to say with certainty, "This is good, this is bad" ? Let us never forget that our notions of good and evil are wholly relative and so ignorant that, in what concerns others, we often find fault with an act which is the expression of a wisdom far greater than our own.

True science does not judge; it investigates phenomena as precisely as it can in their manifold causes and numerous effects. It says, "This will determine that" — see therefore whether *that* conforms to what you wish before doing *this*. At all events, even if in what personally concerns us we can take as a criterion our greater or lesser likeness to our highest ideal in all its intensity and progressive splendour, we have no right to demand from others that they should realise our own ideal, unless we know that our ideal is superior to theirs, in which case we would have to be quite certain that our ideal conforms in every respect to the supreme ideal, the absolute ideal, to the universal plan in its innermost essence....

But before attaining to such transcendent heights, we can always keep in mind that the malevolent or uncharitable thoughts emanating from men are the chief causes of division among them; they make their union almost impossible even when they wish to realise it.

What we constantly endeavour to achieve in our physical actions is at the same time constantly hampered or even destroyed by our mental actions.

So let us watch over our thoughts, let us strive to create for ourselves an atmosphere of beautiful and noble thoughts and we shall have done much to hasten the advent of terrestrial harmony.

19 February 1912

Charity

In its most general sense, charity may be defined as the act of giving to each one what he lacks.

That is to say, in the last analysis, to put each thing in its place, which would result in the establishment of the supreme justice upon earth.

Such is the theory, but in practice charity could be considered as the path men ought to follow in their groping advance towards justice.

For, in his present state of evolution, man is incapable not only of realising justice in his earthly abode, but also of conceiving it as it is in its absolute essence. Charity is the living acknowledgment of this inability.

Indeed, in our ignorance of true justice, the justice which is one with perfect harmony, perfect equilibrium and perfect order, our wisest course is to take the path of love, the path of charity which shuns all judgment.

This is what justifies the attitude of those who always set charity against justice. Justice is, in their eyes, rigorous, merciless, and charity must come to temper its excessive severity.

Certainly, they cannot speak thus of divine justice, but more rightly of human or rather of social justice, the egoistic justice which is instituted to defend a more or less extensive grouping of interests and is as much opposed to true justice as shadow is contrary to light.

When we speak of justice as it is rendered in our so-called civilised countries, we should call it not rigorous and merciless but blind and monstrous in its ignorant pretension.

So we can never make too many amends for its fatal effects, and there charity finds an opportunity to apply itself fruitfully.

But this is only one side of the question and before delving deeper into our subject, I would like to remind you that charity, like all other human activities, is exercised according to four different modes which must be simultaneous if its action is to be integral and truly effective. I mean that no charity is complete if it is not at the same time material, intellectual, spiritual or moral and, above all, loving, for the very essence of charity is love.

At present charity is considered almost exclusively from the external standpoint and the word is synonymous with the sharing of part of one's possessions with life's rejects. We shall see in a moment how mean this conception is even when confined to the purely material field.

The three other modes of action of charity are admirably summed up in this counsel given by the Buddha to his disciples: "With your hearts overflowing with compassion, go forth into this world torn by pain, be instructors, and wherever the darkness of ignorance rules, there light a torch."

To instruct those who know less, to give to those who do evil the strength to come out of their error, to console those who suffer, these are all occupations of charity rightly understood.

Thus charity, regarded from the individual point of view, consists, for each one, of giving to others all they need, in proportion to one's means.

This brings us to two observations.

The first is that one cannot give what one does not have at one's command.

Materially this is so evident that it is unnecessary to insist upon it. But intellectually, spiritually, the same rule holds true.

Indeed, how can one teach others what one does not know ? How can one guide the weak on the path of wisdom if one does not tread the path oneself ? How can one radiate love if one does not possess it within oneself ?

And the supreme charity, which is integral self-giving to the great work of terrestrial regeneration, implies first of all that one can command what one wants to offer, that is to say, that one is master of oneself.

Only he who has perfect self-control can consecrate himself in all sincerity to the great work. For he alone knows that no contrary will, no unexpected impulse can ever again come to impede his action, to check his effort by setting him at variance with himself.

In this fact we find the justification of the old proverb which says: "Charity begins at home."

This maxim seems to encourage every kind of egoism, and yet it is the expression of a great wisdom for one who understands it rightly.

It is because charitable people fail to conform to this principle that their efforts so often remain unfruitful, that their goodwill is so often warped in its results, and that, in the end, they are forced to renounce a charity which, because it has not been rightly exercised, is the cause of nothing but confusion, suffering and disillusionment.

There is evidently a wrong way of interpreting this maxim, which says, "First let us accumulate fortune, intelligence, health, love, energies of all kinds, then we shall distribute them."

For, from the material standpoint, when will the accumulation stop? One who acquires the habit of piling up never finds his pile big enough.

I have even been led to make an observation about this: that in most men generosity seems to exist in inverse proportion to their pecuniary resources.

From observing the way in which workmen, the needy and all the unfortunate act among themselves, I was forced to conclude that the poor are far more charitable, far more prepared to succour their fellow-sufferers than are those more favoured by fortune. There is not enough time to go into the details of all that I have seen, but I assure you that it is instructive. I can, in any case, assure you that if the rich, in proportion to what they have, gave as much as the poor, soon there would no longer be a single starving person in the world.

Thus gold seems to attract gold, and nothing would be more fatal than wanting to accumulate riches before distributing them.

But also, nothing would be more fatal than a rash prodigality which, from lack of discernment, would squander a fortune without benefiting anyone.

Let us never confuse disinterestedness, which is one of the conditions of true charity, with a lack of concern that springs from idle thoughtlessness.

Let us learn therefore to make judicious use of what we may have or earn while giving the least possible play to our personality and, above all, let us not forget that charity should not be confined to material aid.

Nor in the field of forces is it possible to accumulate, for receptivity occurs in proportion to expenditure: the more one expends usefully, the more one makes oneself capable of receiving. Thus the intelligence one can acquire is proportionate to the intelligence one uses. We are formed to manifest a certain quantity of intellectual forces, but if we develop ourselves mentally, if we put our brains to work, if we meditate regularly and above all if we make others benefit by the fruit, however modest, of our efforts, we make ourselves capable of receiving a greater quantity of ever deeper and purer intellectual forces. And the same holds true for love and spirituality.

We are like channels: if we do not allow what they have received to pour out freely, not only do they become blocked and no longer receive anything, but what they contain will spoil. If, on the contrary, we allow all this flood of vital, intellectual and spiritual forces to flow abundantly, if by impersonalising ourselves we know how to connect our little individuality to the great universal current, what we give will be returned to us a hundredfold.

To know how not to cut ourselves off from the great universal current, to be a link in the chain which must not be broken, this is the true science, the very key of charity.

Unfortunately there exists a very widespread error which is a serious obstacle to the practical application of this knowledge. This error lies in the belief that a thing in the universe may

be our own possession. Everything belongs to all, and to say or think, "This is mine", is to create a separation, a division which does not exist in reality.

Everything belongs to all, even the substance of which we are made, a whirl of atoms in perpetual movement which momentarily constitutes our organism without abiding in it and which, tomorrow, will form another.

It is true that some people command great material possessions. But in order to be in accord with the universal law, they should consider themselves as trustees, stewards of these possessions. They ought to know that these riches are entrusted to them so that they may administer them for the best interests of all.

We have come a long way from the narrow conception of charity restricted to the giving of a little of what we have in excess to the unfortunate ones that life brings in our way ! And what we say of material riches must be said of spiritual wealth also.

Those who say, "This idea is mine", and who think they are very charitable in allowing others to profit from it, are senseless.

The world of ideas belongs to all; intellectual force is a universal force.

It is true that some people are more capable than others of entering into relation with this field of ideas and manifesting it through their conscious cerebrality. But this is nothing other than an additional responsibility for them: since they are in possession of this wealth, they are its stewards and must see that it is used for the good of the greatest number.

The same holds true for all the other universal forces. Only the concept of union, of the perfect identity of everything and everyone, can lead to true charity.

But to come back to practice, there is one more serious pitfall in the way of its complete and fruitful manifestation.

For most people, charity consists of giving anything to anyone without even knowing whether this gift corresponds to a need.

97

Thus charity is made synonymous with sentimental weakness and irrational squandering.

Nothing is more contrary to the very essence of this virtue.

Indeed, to give someone a thing he has no need of is as great a lack of charity as to deny him what he needs.

And this applies to the things of the spirit as well as to those of the body.

By a faulty distribution of material possessions one can hasten the downfall of certain individuals by encouraging them to be lazy, instead of favouring their progress by inciting them to effort.

The same holds true for intelligence and love. To give someone a knowledge which is too strong for him, thoughts which he cannot assimilate, is to deprive him for long, if not for ever, of the possibility of thinking for himself.

In the same way, to impose on some people an affection, a love for which they feel no need, is to make them carry a burden which is often too heavy for their shoulders.

This error has two main causes to which all the others can be linked: ignorance and egoism.

In order to be sure that an act is beneficial one must know its immediate or distant consequences, and an act of charity is no exception to this law.

To want to do well is not enough, one must also know.

How much evil has been done in the world in the name of charity diverted from its true sense and completely warped in its results !

I could give you many examples of acts of charity which have led to the most disastrous results because they were performed without reflection, without discernment, without understanding, without insight.

Charity, like all things, must be the result in us of a conscious and reasoned will, for impulse is synonymous with error and above all with egoism.

Unfortunately it must be acknowledged that charity is very

seldom completely disinterested.

I do not mean charity which is performed for the purpose of acquiring merit in the eyes of a personal God or to win eternal bliss.

This utterly base form is the worst of all bargainings and to call it charity would be to tarnish this name.

But I mean charity which is performed because one finds pleasure in it and which is still subject to all kinds of likes or dislikes, attractions or repulsions.

That kind of charity is very rarely completely free from the desire to meet with gratitude, and such a desire always atrophies the impartial clear-sightedness which is necessary to any action if it is to have its full value.

There is a wisdom in charity as everywhere, and it is to reduce waste to the minimum.

Thus to be truly charitable one must be impersonal.

And once more we see that all the lines of human progress converge on the same necessity: self-mastery, dying to oneself in order to be born into the new and true life.

To the extent that we outgrow the habit of referring everything to ourselves, we can exercise a truly effective charity, a charity one with love.

Besides, there is a height where all virtues meet in communion: love, goodness, compassion, forbearance, charity are all one and the same in their essence.

From this point of view, charity could be considered as the tangible and practical outer action determined by the application of the virtues of love.

For there is a force which can be distributed to all, always, provided that it is given in its most impersonal form: this is love, love which contains within itself light and life, that is, all the possibilities of intelligence, health, blossoming.

Yes, there is a sublime charity, one which rises from a happy heart, from a serene soul.

One who has won inner peace is a herald of deliverance

wherever he goes, a bearer of hope and joy. Is not this what poor and suffering humanity needs above all things ?

Yes, there are certain men whose thoughts are all love, who radiate love, and the mere presence of these individuals is a charity more active, more real than any other.

Though they utter no word and make no gesture, yet the sick are relieved, the tormented are soothed, the ignorant are enlightened, the wicked are appeased, those who suffer are consoled and all undergo this deep transformation which will open new horizons to them, enable them to take a step forward which no doubt will be decisive, on the infinite path of progress.

These individuals who, out of love, give themselves to all, who become the servants of all, are the living symbols of the supreme Charity.

I invite all of you here, my brothers, who aspire to be charitable, to join your thought with mine in expressing this wish: that we may strive to follow their example a little more each day so that we may be like them, in the world, messengers of light and love.

20 May 1912

The Divinity Within

All in us that is not wholly consecrated to the Divinity within is in the possession, by fragments, of the whole entirety of things that encompass us and act upon what we improperly call "ourselves", whether through the intermediary of our senses or directly on the mind by suggestion.

The only way to become a conscious being, to be oneself, is to unite with the divine Self that is in all. For that, we must, by the aid of concentration, isolate ourselves from external influences.

When you are one with the Divinity within, you are one with all things in their depths. And it is through It and by It that you must enter into relation with them. You are then, but without attraction or repulsion, near to whatever is near to It and far from whatever is far.

Living among others you should always be a divine example, an occasion offered to them to understand and to enter on the path of the life divine. Nothing more: you should not even have the desire to make them progress; for that too would be something arbitrary.

Until you are definitively one with the Divinity within, the best way, in your relations with the outside, is to act according to the unanimous advice given by those who have themselves had the experience of this unity.

To be in a state of constant benevolence, with this as your rule, not to be troubled by anything and not to be the cause of trouble to others, not to inflict suffering upon them so far as possible.

8 June 1912

PART 4

Essays, letters, etc. written in Japan between 1916 and 1920

PART 1

Woman and the War

You have asked me what I think of the feminist movement and what will be the consequences of the present war for it.

One of the first effects of the war has certainly been to give quite a new aspect to the question. The futility of the perpetual oppositions between men and women was at once made clearly apparent, and behind the conflict of the sexes, only relating to exterior facts, the gravity of the circumstances allowed the discovery of the always existent, if not always outwardly manifested fact, of the real collaboration, of the true union of these two complementary halves of humanity.

Many men were surprised to see how easily women could replace them in most of the posts they occupied before, and to their surprise was added something of regret not to have found sooner a real partner of their work and their struggles in her whom more often they had only considered as an object of pleasure and distraction, or at best as the guardian of their hearth and mother of their children. Certainly woman is that and to be it well requires exceptional qualities, but she is not only that, as the present circumstances have amply proved.

In going to tend the wounded in the most difficult material conditions, actually under the enemy's fire, the so-called weak sex has proved that its physical energy and power of endurance were equal to those of man. But where, above all, women have given proof of exceptional gifts is in their organising faculties. These faculties of administration were recognised in them long ago by the Brahmanic India of before the Mohammedan conquest. There is a popular adage there which says: "Property governed by woman means prosperous property." But in the Occident Semitic thought allied to Roman legislation has influenced customs too deeply for women to have the opportunity of showing their capacity for organisation.

It is true that in France one frequently sees the woman absolute mistress of the administration of her house even from the pecuniary point of view, and the so proverbial riches of the French *petite bourgeoisie* proves that the system has a good side. It was rare however to see the feminine faculties utilised to direct undertakings of great importance, and until now the confidential posts of public administration had always been closed to them. The present war has shown that in refusing the co-operation of women the governments deprived themselves of precious help. I will cite you an event as example.

A few months after the outbreak of the war, when the Germans had almost entirely occupied the Belgian territory, the inhabitants of the invaded regions were in indescribable misery. Fortunately, thanks to the initiative of several rich American men and women, a Society was founded to supply the most urgent needs of the sorely tried populations. As the result of certain military operations a fairly large group of small villages were suddenly deprived of all food. Famine was imminent. The American Society sent a message to some similar English Societies asking that five vans of the most indispensable supplies should be dispatched immediately. These vans must reach their destination in three days. The men to whom this request was addressed replied that it was quite impossible to comply with it. Luckily a woman heard of the matter. It seemed terrible to her that in such tragic circumstances one could use the word "impossible". She belonged to a group of women who aided the wounded and sufferers of the war. Immediately they promised the American Society they would satisfy it and in three days the numerous obstacles were overcome though some of the difficulties, especially those concerning transport, seemed truly unsurmountable. A powerful organising mind, an ardent will, had done the miracle: the provisions arrived in time and the dreadful misery of famine was thus avoided.

This is not to say that only woman's exceptional qualities have been revealed by the present war. Her weaknesses, her

faults, her pettiness have also been given the opportunity of display, and certainly if women wish to take the place they claim
in the governing of nations they must progress much further in
the mastery of self, the broadening of ideas and points of view,
in intellectual suppleness and oblivion of their sentimental preferences in order to become worthy of the management of public affairs.

It is certain that purely masculine politics have given proof
of incapacity; they have foundered too often in their search of
strictly personal interest, and in their arbitrary and violent action. Doubtless women's politics would bring about a tendency
to disinterestedness and more humanitarian solutions. But unfortunately, in their present state, women in general are creatures
of passion and enthusiastic partisanship; they lack the reasoning
calm that purely intellectual activity gives; the latter is undoubtedly dangerous because hard and cold and pitiless, nevertheless it is unquestionably useful to master the overflow of
sentiment which cannot hold a predominant place in the ruling
of collective interests.

These faults which would be serious if the activity of women
had to replace that of men, could form, on the contrary, by a
collaboration of the two sexes, an element of compensation for
the opposite faults of men. That would be the best means of
leading them gradually to mutual perfecting. To reduce the woman's part to solely interior and domestic occupations, and the
man's part to exclusively exterior and social occupations, thus
separating what should be united, would be to perpetuate the
present sad state of things, from which both are equally suffering. It is in front of the highest duties and heaviest responsibilities that their respective qualities must unite in a close and con-
fident solidarity.

Is it not time that this hostile attitude of the two sexes facing
one another as irreconcilable adversaries should cease ? A severe,
a painful lesson is being given to the nations. On the ruins piled
up now, new constructions more beautiful and more harmonious

107

can be erected. It is no longer the moment for frail competitions and self-interested claims; all human beings, men or women, must associate in a common effort to become conscious of the highest ideal which asks to be realised and to work ardently for its realisation. The question to be solved, the real question is then not only that of a better utilisation of their outer activities, but above all that of an inner spiritual growth. Without inner progress there is no possible outer progress.

Thus the problem of feminism, as all the problems of the world, comes back to a spiritual problem. For the spiritual reality is at the basis of all others; the divine world, the Dhammata of Buddhism, is the eternal foundation on which are built all the other worlds. In regard to this Supreme Reality all are equal, men and women, in rights and in duties; the only distinction which can exist in this domain being based on the sincerity and ardour of aspiration, on the constancy of the will. And it is in the recognition of this fundamental spiritual equality that can be found the only serious and lasting solution for this problem of the relation of the sexes. It is in this light that it must be placed, it is at this height that must be sought the focus of action and new life, around which will be constructed the future temple of Humanity.

7 July 1916

Woman and Man

Let us first take for granted that pride and impudence are always ridiculous: only stupid and ignorant people are arrogant. As soon as a human being is sufficiently enlightened to have a contact, however slight, with the all-pervading mystery of the universe, he becomes necessarily humble.

Woman, by the very fact of her passivity, having more easily than man the intuition of the Supreme Power at work in the world, is more often, more naturally humble.

But to base the fact of this humility on need is erroneous. Woman needs man not more than man needs woman; or rather, more exactly, man and woman have an equal need of one another.

Even in the mere material domain, there are as many men who depend materially upon women as there are women who depend upon men. If humility were a result of that dependency, then, in the first case, the men ought to be humble and the women to have the authority.

Besides, to say that women should be humble because it is thus that they please men, is also erroneous. It would lead one to think that woman has been put on earth only for the purpose of giving pleasure to man — which is absurd.

All the universe has been created to express the Divine Power, and human beings, men or women, have for special mission to become conscious of and to manifest that Eternal Divine Essence. Such is their object and none other. And if they knew and remembered that more often, men and women would cease to think of petty quarrels about priority or authority; they would not see a greater mark of respect in the fact of being served than of serving, for all would consider themselves equally as servitors of the Divine, and would make it their honour to serve ever more and ever better.

Impressions of Japan

You ask me for my impressions about Japan. To write on Japan is a difficult task; so many things have been already written, so many silly things also... but these more on the people than on their country. For the country is so wonderful, picturesque, many-sided, unexpected, charming, wild or sweet; it is in its appearance so much a synthesis of all the other countries of the world, from the tropical to the arctic, that no artistic eye can remain indifferent to it. I believe many excellent descriptions have been given of Japan; I shall not then attempt to add mine, which would certainly be far less interesting. But the people of Japan have, in general, been misunderstood and misinterpreted, and on that subject something worth saying remains to be said.

In most cases foreigners come in touch with that part of the Japanese people which has been spoiled by foreigners, — a Japan of money-makers and imitators of the West; obviously they have proved very clever imitators, and you can easily find here a great many of those things which make the West hateful. If we judge Japan by her statesmen, her politicians and her businessmen, we shall find her a country very much like one of the Powers of Europe, though she possesses the vitality and concentrated energies of a nation which has not yet reached its zenith.

That energy is one of the most interesting features of Japan. It is visible everywhere, in everyone; the old and the young, the workmen, the women, the children, the students, all, save perhaps the "new rich", display in their daily life the most wonderful storage of concentrated energy. With their perfect love for nature and beauty, this accumulated strength is, perhaps, the most distinctive and widely spread characteristic of the Japanese. That is what you may observe as soon as you reach that land of the Rising Sun where so many people and so many treasures are gathered in a narrow island.

But if you have — as we have had — the privilege of coming in contact with the true Japanese, those who kept untouched the righteousness and bravery of the ancient Samurai, then you can understand what in truth is Japan, you can seize the secret of her force. They know how to remain silent; and though they are possessed of the most acute sensitiveness, they are, among the people I have met, those who express it the least. A friend here can give his life with the greatest simplicity to save yours, though he never told you before he loved you in such a profound and unselfish way. Indeed he had not even told you that he had loved you at all. And if you were not able to read the heart behind the appearances, you would have seen only a very exquisite courtesy which leaves little room for the expression of spontaneous feelings. Nevertheless the feelings are there, all the stronger perhaps because of the lack of outward manifestation; and if an opportunity presents itself, through an act, very modest and veiled sometimes, you suddenly discover depths of affection.

This is specifically Japanese; among the nations of the world, the true Japanese — those who have not become westernised — are perhaps the least selfish. And this unselfishness is not the privilege of the well-educated, the learned or the religious people; in all social ranks you may find it. For here, with the exception of some popular and exceedingly pretty festivals, religion is not a rite or a cult, it is a daily life of abnegation, obedience, self-sacrifice.

The Japanese are taught from their infancy that life is duty and not pleasure. They accept that duty — so often hard and painful — with passive submission. They are not tormented by the idea of making themselves happy. It gives to the life of the whole country a very remarkable self-constraint, but no joyful and free expansion; it creates an atmosphere of tension and effort, of mental and nervous strain, not of spiritual peace like that which can be felt in India, for instance. Indeed, nothing in

111

Japan can be compared to the pure divine atmosphere which pervades India and makes of her such a unique and precious country; not even in the temples and the sacred monasteries always so wonderfully situated, sometimes on the summit of a high mountain covered with huge cedar trees, difficult to reach, far from the world below.... Exterior calm, rest and silence are there, but not that blissful sense of the infinite which comes from a living nearness to the Unique. True, here all speaks to the eyes and mind of unity — unity of God with man, unity of man with Nature, unity of man with man. But this unity is very little felt and lived. Certainly the Japanese have a highly developed sense of generous hospitality, reciprocal help, mutual support; but in their feelings, their thoughts, their actions in general, they are among the most individualist, the most separatist people. For them the form is predominant, the form is attractive. It is suggestive too, it speaks of some deeper harmony or truth, of some law of nature or life. Each form, each act is symbolical, from the arrangement of the gardens and the houses to the famous tea ceremony. And sometimes in a very simple and usual thing you discover a symbol, deep, elaborated, willed, that most of the people know and understand; but it is an exterior and learnt knowledge — a tradition, it is not living truth coming from the depth of spiritual experience, enlightening heart and mind. Japan is essentially the country of sensations; she lives through her eyes. Beauty rules over her as an uncontested master; and all her atmosphere incites to mental and vital activity, study, observation, progress, effort, not to silent and blissful contemplation. But behind this activity stands a high aspiration which the future of her people will reveal.

9 July 1917

112

The Children of Japan

In my last letter[1] I spoke of the sense of duty which gave to the Japanese people a great self-constraint, but no joyful and free expansion. I must make an exception to this rule and this exception is in favour of the children.

We could quite well call Japan the paradise of children — in no other country I have seen them so free and so happy. After months of residence in Japan I have yet never seen a child beaten by a grown-up person. They are treated as if all the parents were conscious that the children are the promise and the glory of the future. And a wonderful thing is that, environed by so much attention, so much care, — indeed, such a devotion, they are the most reasonable, good and serious children I have ever met. When they are babies, tied up in an amusing fashion on their mothers' backs, with their wide open black eyes they seem to consider life with gravity and to have already opinions on the things they look at. You scarcely hear a child cry. When, for instance, he has hurt himself and the tears burst out of his eyes, the mother or the father has but to say a few words in a low voice, and the sorrow seems to be swept away. What are those magic words which enable children to be so reasonable ? Very simple indeed: "Are you not a Samurai ?" And this question is sufficient for the child to call to him all his energy and to overcome his weakness.

In the streets you see hundreds of children, in their charming bright "*kimono*",[2] playing freely, in spite of the "*kuruma*"[3] and the bicycles, at the most inventive and picturesque games, pleased with little, singing and laughing.

When older, but still very young, you may see them in the tram cars, dressed with foreign clothes, the student cap on the

[1] I.e., "Impressions of Japan".
[2] Traditional wide-sleeved gown.
[3] A word applied to many vehicles, here probably a carriage or a rickshaw.

113

head, the knapsack on the back, proud of their importance, still prouder at the idea of all they are learning and will learn. For they love their studies and are the most earnest students. They never miss an opportunity of adding something to their growing knowledge; and when the work for the school leaves them some liberty they occupy it in reading books. The young Japanese seem to have a real passion for books. In Tokyo one of the main streets is nearly entirely occupied by secondhand book-sellers. From the beginning to the end of the year these shops are full of students, and it is not often novels they are seeking for !

They are, as a rule, very anxious to learn foreign languages and when they come to meet foreigners, though they are in general very timid, they make use of that acquaintance as much as they can to...[1]

A country where such are the children and so they are treated is a country still ascending the steps of progress and of mastery.

---

[1] This sentence was left incomplete.

114

To the Women of Japan

To speak of children to the women of Japan is, I think, to speak to them of their dearest, their most sacred subject. Indeed, in no other country in the world have the children taken such an important, such a primordial place. They are, here, the centre of care and attention. On them are concentrated — and rightly — the hopes for the future. They are the living promise of growing prosperity for the country. Therefore, the most important work assigned to women in Japan is child-making. Maternity is considered as the principal role of woman. But this is true only so long as we understand what is meant by the word maternity. For to bring children into the world as rabbits do their young — instinctively, ignorantly, machine-like, that certainly cannot be called maternity ! True maternity begins with the conscious creation of a being, with the willed shaping of a soul coming to develop and utilise a new body. The true domain of women is the spiritual. We forget it but too often.

To bear a child and construct his body almost subconsciously is not enough. The work really commences when, by the power of thought and will, we conceive and create a character capable of manifesting an ideal.

And do not say that we have no power for realising such a thing. Innumerable instances of this very effective power could be brought out as proofs.

First of all, the effect of physical environment was recognised and studied long ago. It is by surrounding women with forms of art and beauty that, little by little, the ancient Greeks created the exceptionally harmonious race that they were.

Individual instances of the same fact are numerous. It is not rare to see a woman who, while pregnant, had looked at constantly and admired a beautiful picture or statue, giving birth to a child after the perfect likeness of this picture or statue. I met several of these instances myself. Among them, I remember

115

very clearly two little girls; they were twins and perfectly beautiful. But the most astonishing was how little like their parents they were. They reminded me of a very famous picture painted by the English artist Reynolds. One day I made this remark to the mother, who immediately exclaimed: "Indeed, is it not so? You will be interested to know that while I was expecting these children, I had, hanging above my bed, a very good reproduction of Reynolds' picture. Before going to sleep and as soon as I woke, my last and first glance was for that picture; and in my heart I hoped: may my children be like the faces in this picture. You see that I succeeded quite well!" In truth, she could be proud of her success, and her example is of great utility for other women.

But if we can obtain such results on the physical plane where the materials are the least plastic, how much more so on the psychological plane where the influence of thought and will is so powerful. Why accept the obscure bonds of heredity and atavism — which are nothing else than subconscious preferences for our own trend of character — when we can, by concentration and will, call into being a type constructed according to the highest ideal we are able to conceive? With this effort, maternity becomes truly precious and sacred; indeed with this, we enter the glorious work of the Spirit, and womanhood rises above animality and its ordinary instincts, towards real humanity and its powers.

In this effort, in this attempt, then, lies our true duty. And if this duty was always of the greatest importance, it certainly has taken a capital one in the present turn of the earth's evolution.

For we are living in an exceptional time at an exceptional turning point of the world's history. Never before, perhaps, did mankind pass through such a dark period of hatred, bloodshed and confusion. And, at the same time, never had such a strong, such an ardent hope awakened in the hearts of the people. Indeed, if we listen to our heart's voice, we immediately perceive that we are, more or less consciously, waiting for a new reign of justice, of beauty, of harmonious good-will and fraternity. And this seems in complete contradiction with the actual state of the world. But we all know that never is the night so dark as before the dawn. May not this darkness, then, be the sign of an approaching dawn ? And as never was night so complete, so terrifying, maybe never will dawn have been so bright, so pure, so illuminating as the coming one.... After the bad dreams of the night the world will awaken to a new consciousness.

The civilisation which is ending now in such a dramatic way was based on the power of mind, mind dealing with matter and life. What it has been to the world, we have not to discuss here. But a new reign is coming, that of the Spirit: after the human, the divine.

Yet, if we have been fortunate enough to live on earth at such a stupendous, a unique time as this one, is it sufficient to stand and watch the unfolding events ? All those who feel that their heart extends further than the limits of their own person and family, that their thought embraces more than small personal interests and local conventions, all those, in short, who realise that they belong not to themselves, or to their family, or even to their country, but to God who manifests Himself in all countries, through mankind, these, indeed, know that they must rise and set to work for the sake of humanity, for the advent of the Dawn.

And in this momentous, endless, many-sided work, what can be the part of womanhood ? It is true that, as soon as great events and works are in question, the custom is to relegate women to a corner with a smile of patronising contempt which means: this is not your business, poor, feeble, futile creatures.... And women, submissive, childlike, lazy perhaps, have accepted, at least in many countries, this deplorable state of things. I dare to say that they are wrong. In the life of the future, there shall be no more room for such division, such disequilibrium between the masculine and the feminine. The true relation of the two sexes is an equal footing of mutual help and close collaboration.

And from now, we must reassume our veritable position, take again our due place and assert our real importance — that of spiritual former and educator. Indeed, some men, perhaps a little vainglorious of their so-called advantages, may despise the apparent weakness of women (although even this exterior weakness is not quite certain) but: "Do what he may, the superman will have to be born of woman all the same", someone said very rightly.

The superman shall be born of woman, this is a big unquestionable truth; but it is not enough to be proud of this truth, we must clearly understand what it means, become aware of the responsibility it creates, and learn to face earnestly the task which is put before us. This task is precisely our most important share in the present world-wide work.

For that, we must first understand — at least in their broad lines — what are the means by which the present chaos and obscurity can be transformed into light and harmony.

Many means have been suggested: political, social, ethical, even religious.... Indeed, none of these seem sufficient to face with any reliable success the magnitude of the task to be done. Only a new spiritual influx, creating in man a new consciousness, can overcome the enormous mass of difficulties barring the way of the workers. A new spiritual light, a manifestation upon earth of some divine force unknown until now, a Thought of God, new for us, descending into this world and taking a new form here.

And here we come back to our starting point, to our duty of true maternity. For this form meant to manifest the spiritual force capable of transforming the earth's present conditions, this new form, who is to construct it if not the women?

Thus we see that at this critical period of the world's life it is no longer sufficient to give birth to a being in whom our highest personal ideal is manifested; we must strive to find out what is the future type, whose advent Nature is planning. It is no longer sufficient to form a man similar to the greatest men we

118

have heard of or known, or even greater, more accomplished and gifted than they; we must strive to come in touch mentally, by the constant aspiration of our thought and will, with the supreme possibility which, exceeding all human measures and features, will give birth to the superman.

Once again Nature feels one of her great impulses towards the creation of something utterly new, something unexpected. And it is to this impulse that we must answer and obey.

Let us try first to discover where this impulse of Nature will lead us. And the best way for that is to look back on the lessons given to us by the Past.

We see that each progress of Nature, each manifestation of a new capacity and principle upon earth is marked by the appearance of a new species. In the same way, the progressive forms of the life of races, of peoples, of individuals, follow each other through the human cycles, ceaselessly inspired, fecundated, renewed by the efforts of the guides of humanity. And all these forms aim at the same goal, the mysterious, the glorious goal of Nature.[1]

It is to this call of Nature that we must answer, to this mag-

---

[1] *It seems that the following paragraphs from an earlier draft were intended for insertion here:*

Which is this goal ? Toward what unexpected realisation of the future does Nature aim ? What does she seek since her dark origins ?

Each form that she creates is a fresh affirmation of that which through her will be born, of that which it is her mission to manifest.

Each species preparing the others, making them possible, bears witness to her untiring perseverance, is a proof of her solemn vow; in each one is a little more matter transfigured, announcing future dawns of intelligence. Through innumerable cycles how many paths has she had to follow in order to reach at last the cave of the anthropoid, the primitive man ?

It is before him that will open the royal avenue leading to the palace of spirit. But how many races, how many generations will pass on the earth without discovering it, how many wrong paths will Nature follow in the footsteps of man. For, believing himself the masterpiece of the universe, he knows not that he has a further stage to pass through.

Could the idea of man be conceived, before he existed, in the obscure brain of even the nearest of his ancestors ? Can the idea of the superman, before he exists, penetrate into the brain of man ?

And yet, in every child of man which comes into the world, in every

---

nificent, to this grandiose work that we must devote ourselves. Let us try to make as clear as we can the steps of our advance on this difficult and as yet unexplored path.

First of all we must be careful, in our attempt to conceive the future man or superman, not to adopt an actual type of man, perfecting or aggrandising him. To avoid as much as possible this mistake we should study the teachings of life's evolution.

We have already seen that the appearance of a new species always announces the manifestation on earth of a new principle,

---

growing intelligence, in every effort of the emerging generations, in every attempt of human genius, Nature seeks the way which, once again, will lead her further.

Fifteen hundred million men since perhaps fifteen hundred centuries wander without finding this way.

Among the multitude of the ways over which all the efforts of their progress are scattered, in this domain as in all the others, only one is good: it is the way of synthetic perfections. Where to discover it ?

And who among men dares to venture elsewhere than on the easy and well-beaten tracks ? Who, knowing that there is another path which goes further, accepts to lose all in order to find it perhaps, to lose all in walking alone, in thinking alone, always apart among the others, not even certain of attaining what he seeks.

Try not to discover this one among the men who excel and shine, for these excel and shine only in being, somewhat more perfectly, similar to their own kind.

Precious stones also excel and shine among all the other stones, but the most beautiful gem is outside the series of chemical combinations from whence comes forth life. In the same way, ascending the series of forms, the most beautiful tree of the forest is outside the lines of evolution which lead the biological process up to the animal, up to man.

And once again, among men, the most admired, the most famous, the most artistic, the most learned, the most religious, may well find himself far off the way leading from man to superman.

Each race, each civilisation, each human society, each religion, represents a new attempt of Nature, one more effort adding to the long series of those she multiplied during countless time.

Now, as among all the animal forms there was one from which man was to come forth, so also, among the social and religious species, must one be born from which some day will come forth the superman.

For it is this which Nature seeks in all her successive attempts, from the first germination of life until man, until the God who shall be born of him.

In the multitude of men she seeks the possibility of the superman; and in each one of them, she aims towards the realisation of the divine.

a new plane of consciousness, a new force or power. But, at the same time, while the new species acquires this formerly unmanifested power or consciousness, it may lose one or many of the perfections which were the characteristics of the immediately preceding species. For instance, to speak only of the last step of Nature's development, what are the greatest differences between man and his immediate predecessor, the ape ? In the monkey we see vitality and physical ability reaching the utmost perfection, a perfection that the new species had to abandon. For man, there has been no more of that marvellous climbing up trees, somersaults over abysses, jumps from summit to summit, but in exchange he acquired intelligence, the power of reasoning, combining, constructing. Indeed with man it is the life of mind, of intellect which appeared on earth. Man is essentially a mental being; and if his possibilities do not stop there, if he feels in himself other worlds, other faculties, other planes of consciousness beyond his mental life, they are only as promises for the future, in the same way as the mental possibilities are latent in the monkey.

It is true that some men, very few, have lived in that world beyond, which we may call the spiritual; some have been, indeed, the living incarnations of that world on earth, but they are the exceptions, the forerunners showing the way to the race, leading it towards its future realisation, not the average man. But that which was the privilege of a few beings scattered through time and space, shall become the central characteristic of the new type which is to appear.

At present, man governs his life through reason; all the activities of the mind are of common use for him; his means of knowledge are observation and deduction; it is by and through reasoning that he takes his decision and chooses his way — or believes he does — in life.

The new race shall be governed by intuition, that is to say, direct perception of the divine law within. Some human beings actually know and experience intuition — as, undoubtedly, certain big gorillas of the forests have glimpses of reasoning.

In mankind, the very few who have cultivated their inner self, who have concentrated their energies on the discovery of the true law of their being, possess more or less the faculty of intuition. When the mind is perfectly silent, pure like a well-polished mirror, immobile as a pond on a breezeless day, then, from above, as the light of the stars drops in the motionless waters, so the light of the supermind, of the Truth within, shines in the quieted mind and gives birth to intuition. Those who are accustomed to listen to this voice out of the Silence, take it more and more as the instigating motive of their actions; and where others, the average men, wander along the intricate paths of reasoning, they go straight their way, guided through the windings of life by intuition, this superior instinct, as by a strong and unfailing hand.

This faculty which is exceptional, almost abnormal now, will certainly be quite common and natural for the new race, the man of tomorrow. But probably the constant exercise of it will be detrimental to the reasoning faculties. As man possesses no more the extreme physical ability of the monkey, so also will the superman lose the extreme mental ability of man,[1] this ability to deceive himself and others.

Thus, man's road to supermanhood will be open when he declares boldly that all he has yet developed, including the intellect of which he is so rightly and yet so vainly proud, is now no longer sufficient for him, and that to uncase, discover, set free this greater power within, shall be henceforward his great preoccupation. Then will his philosophy, art, science, ethics, social existence, vital pursuits be no longer an exercise of mind and life for themselves, in a circle, but a means for the discovery of a greater Truth behind mind and life and the bringing of its power into our human existence. And this discovery is that of

---

[1] *Alternative ending (from earlier draft)*: perhaps all of the power of reasoning; and, even, the organ itself may become useless, disappear little by little as the monkey's tail, which was of no use for man, disappeared from his physical body.

our real, because our highest self and nature.

However, that self which we are not yet, but have to become, is not the strong vital Will hymned by Nietzsche, but a spiritual self and spiritual nature. For as soon as we speak of supermanhood we must be careful to avoid all confusion with the strong but so superficial and incomplete conception of Nietzsche's superman.

Indeed, since Nietzsche invented the word superman, when someone uses it to speak of the coming race, willingly or not, it evokes at the same time Nietzsche's conception. Certainly, his idea that to develop the superman out of our present very unsatisfactory manhood is our real business, is in itself an absolutely sound idea; certainly, his formula of our aim, "to become ourselves", implying, as it does, that man has not yet found all his true self, his true nature by which he can successfully and spontaneously live, could not be bettered; nevertheless, Nietzsche made the mistake we said we ought to avoid: his superman is but a man aggrandised, magnified, in whom Force has become super-dominant, crushing under its weight all the other attributes of man. Such cannot be our ideal. We see too well at present whither leads the exclusive worshipping of Force — to the crimes of the strong and the ruin of continents.

No, the way to supermanhood lies in the unfolding of the ever-perfect Spirit. All would change, all would become easy if man could once consent to be spiritualised. The higher perfection of the spiritual life will come by a spontaneous obedience of spiritualised man to the truth of his own realised being, when he has become himself, found his own real nature; but this spontaneity will not be instinctive and subconscient as in the animal, but intuitive and fully, integrally conscient.

Therefore, the individuals who will most help the future of humanity in the new age, will be those who will recognise a spiritual evolution as the destiny and therefore the great need of the human being, an evolution or conversion of the present type of humanity into a spiritualised humanity, even as the animal man has been largely converted into a highly mentalised humanity.

They will be comparatively indifferent to particular belief and form of religion, and leave men to resort to the beliefs and forms to which they are naturally drawn. They will only hold as essential the faith in the spiritual conversion. They will especially not make the mistake of thinking that this change can be effected by machinery and outward institutions; they will know and never forget that it has to be lived out by each man inwardly or it can never be made a reality.

And among these individuals, woman must be the first to realise this great change, as it is her special task to give birth in this world to the first specimens of the new race. And to be able to do this she must, more or less, conceive what will be the practical results of this spiritual conversion. For if it cannot be effected simply by exterior transformations, it can neither be realised without bringing forth such transformations.

These will certainly not be less in the moral and social domains than in the intellectual.

As religious beliefs and cults will become secondary, so also the ethical restrictions or prescriptions, rules of conduct or conventions will lose their importance.[1]

---

[1] *This paragraph and the two which precede it replace the following passage of an earlier draft:*

But among these individuals woman, as we have already said, will have one special task to accomplish, that of giving birth in this world to the first specimens of the new race. And to be able to do this we must, more or less, conceive first in our thought the ideal of what the superman can be.

Of course, nothing is more difficult than to draw a picture of what will be the new race; it is an almost unrealisable attempt, and we shall certainly not try to enter into details; for we cannot ask of our mind to grasp with any certainty or accuracy this creation of the supermind, of the spirit.

But as we have already seen that the replacing of mental reason by intuitive knowledge will be one of the characteristic features of the future being, in the same way, morally and socially what can be the standard of the new race's life ?

From the ethical point of view, for the individual of the new race there will certainly be no more restrictions or prescriptions, rules of conduct or conventions.

Actually, in human life, the whole moral problem is concentrated in the conflict between the vital will with its impulses and the mental power with its decrees. When the vital will is submitted to the mental power, then the life of the individual or of the society becomes moral. But it is only when both, vital will and mental power, are equally submissive to something higher, to the supermind, that human life is exceeded, that true spiritual life begins, the life of the superman; for his law will come from within, it will be the divine law shining in the centre of each being and governing life from therein, the divine law multiple in its manifestation but one in its origin. And because of its unity this law is the law of supreme order and harmony.

Thus the individual, no more guided by egoistical motives, laws or customs, shall abandon all selfish aims. His rule will be perfect disinterestedness. To act in view of a personal profit, either in this world or in another beyond, will become an unthinkable impossibility. For each act will be done in complete, simple, joyful obedience to the divine law which inspires it, without any seeking for reward or results, as the supreme reward will be in the very delight of acting under such inspiration, of being identified in conscience and will with the divine principle within oneself.

And in this identification the superman will find also his social standard. For in discovering the divine law in himself he will recognise the same divine law in every being, and by being identified with it in himself he will be identified with it in all, thus becoming aware of the unity of all, not only in essence and substance but also in the most exterior planes of life and form. He will not be a mind, a life or a body, but the informing and sustaining Soul or Self, silent, peaceful, eternal, that possesses them; and this Soul or Self he will find everywhere sustaining and informing and possessing all lives and minds and bodies. He will be conscious of this Self as the divine creator and doer of all works, one in all existences; for the many souls of the universal manifestation are only faces of the one Divine. He will

125

perceive each being to be the universal Divinity presenting to him many faces; he will merge himself in That and perceive his own mind, life and body as only one presentation of the Self, and all whom we, at present, conceive of as others will be to his consciousness his own self in other minds, lives and bodies. He will be able to feel his body one with all bodies, as he will be aware constantly of the unity of all matter; he will unite himself in mind and heart with all existences; in short, he will see and feel his own person in all others and all others in himself, realising thus true solidarity in the perfection of unity.

But we must limit to these indispensable hints our description of the superman, and push no further our attempt to picture him, as we are convinced that any endeavour to be more precise would prove not only vain but useless. For it is not a number of imaginings, more or less exact, which can help us in the formation of the future type. It is by holding firm in our heart and mind the dynamism, the irresistible impetus given by a sincere and ardent aspiration, by maintaining in ourselves a certain state of enlightened receptivity towards the supreme Idea of the new race which wills to be manifested on earth, that we can take a decisive step in the formation of the sons of the future, and make ourselves fit to serve as intermediaries for the creation of those who shall save Humanity.[1]

---

[1] *Alternate ending (from an earlier draft):* of the saviours of the world. *The earlier draft closes with the following additional paragraph:*

For, in truth, saviours they will be, as each being of this new type will not live either for himself or for State or society, for the individual ego or the collective ego, but for something much greater, for God in himself and for God in the world.